"There are th_____ _____ ____ I cannot explain. The drive. The desire . . . One night, a guy puts a gun in my side and says, 'Don't move.' He takes the wallet. I try to stand up, but three hours out there playing decoy, lying on the sidewalk pretending to be a bum, and my legs are gone. So I jump on the hood of a cab and we go after the guy. The cab catches up with the guy, but he stops short and I go flying . . . The cops have the prisoner at gunpoint, but somehow he gets away, he starts running. I see this, and even though I'm lying in my own blood, I get up and go after him."

THE SYSTEM . . .

"I'd see these cops in their cars, studying for the sergeant's test. One time a ten-thirteen comes over the radio and I see this guy and he doesn't even lay down the book. A ten-thirteen! Another cop in trouble! I took my radio car and smashed into the back of his cruiser. I yelled over, 'You ———, get your ass moving or I will personally rip off your nose.' Some of these hairbags wound up as sergeants and lieutenants and captains."

THE MAN WHO BECAME A LEGEND . . .

ONE TOUGH COP

ONE TOUCH COP

The Bo Dietl Story

BO DIETL and KEN CROSS

With an Introduction by
Nicholas Pileggi

POCKET BOOKS

New York   London   Toronto   Sydney   Tokyo   Singapore

Thanks, Joyce Seymour
—Ken Gross

An *Original* publication of POCKET BOOKS

 POCKET BOOKS, a division of Simon & Schuster Inc.
1230 Avenue of the Americas, New York, NY 10020

Copyright © 1988 by Richard "Bo" Dietl and Ken Gross
Introduction copyright © 1988 by Nicholas Pileggi

ISBN: 0-671-02841-3

First Pocket Books printing August 1988

10 9 8 7 6 5 4 3

POCKET and colophon are registered trademarks of
Simon & Schuster Inc.

Printed in the U.S.A.

Quote from the *New York Daily News* on page 30: © 1981 New York
News Inc. Reprinted with permission.

To my father

I only got to know him after I became a man
but I couldn't have gotten there
without his help.

To my mom

The only person who was there,
all the time
when I needed her.

Introduction

Until his retirement in 1985 at the age of thirty-five, Richard "Bo" Dietl was probably the best detective in New York. He was certainly one of the city's most decorated cops, having received over seventy-five police department medals and awards and dozens of public service and community awards. But, in addition to making arrests and getting convictions against hundreds of stickup men and street muggers, Dietl specialized in tracking down the kinds of murderers and rapists who almost got away.

It was Dietl, for instance, who pursued the two men who raped and tortured a thirty-year-old nun in an East Harlem, Manhattan, convent in 1981. Both men later confessed.

It was also Dietl who found the man who was later convicted of the Palm Sunday Massacre, the city's bloodiest mass slaying, in which ten people—eight children, ages three to twelve, and two women, twenty-one and twenty-four—were found shot to death in various rooms of their East New York apartment.

Yet, while Dietl has been credited with solving some of the city's most publicized crimes, most of the arrests he made never got in the newspapers or on the six o'clock news.

From his first day as a probationary patrolman, when he ran across rooftops chasing a burglar, Dietl just loved catching crooks. Shortly after his graduation from the police academy in 1971, Dietl volunteered for the super active Citywide Anti-Crime Squad where, during most of his fifteen-year career, he made over 1400 felony arrests—the average cop makes 180 during the same career span—and had a phenomenal ninety-five percent conviction rate. He has been mugged over 500 times while assigned to the decoy unit where he specialized in the role of a drowsy or drunken commuter. He has been rushed to hospital emergency wards more than a dozen times. He has been stabbed, shot at, beaten, run over and pushed down flights of subway stairs. And yet, despite innumerable incidents of provocation in which Dietl's challengers had to be subdued, the five-foot-eight-inch, 190-pound physical fitness buff (he is the police department's unofficial arm-wrestling champ) never once fired his gun at a suspect.

Dietl, however, like many great street cops, was never very good at playing departmental politics. He was the kind of traditional cop who preferred working the streets and making arrests to taking civil service tests toward promotion. He complained a lot about how the city's prosecutors tried to water down his cases in court and he thought nothing of storming into a supervisor's office or threatening to go to the press. He made arrests on his days off and he drove some of the department's nine-to-five desk officers crazy having to process his paperwork when he wasn't even on duty. To the police brass downtown, Dietl was the closest thing New York had to Dirty Harry.

During his first year as a uniformed recruit in Queens, Dietl amazed his precinct superiors by making dozens of arrests of the pill and pot pushers around the schools and playgrounds on his neighborhood beat. When they realized he was cleaning up his beat of drug pushers by taking off his uniform hat and jacket and donning a Day-Glo sweatshirt and dark glasses, he was reprimanded and ordered to wear his hat and uniform jacket when on duty. Dietl then began making the arrests on his own time. Dietl, in other words, was the kind of cop who never let the department's 1500 pages of rules and regulations get in the way of his job.

But, while Dietl's aggressive style helped him clean up his beat and catch crooks, it also antagonized his superiors, and it was one of the reasons he remained an anti-crime street cop for thirteen years, when anyone else with his record of arrests and convictions would have been promoted to the elite detective division years earlier.

For instance, when Dietl caught the two hoods who raped the nun, he wasn't even supposed to be working on the case.

Nevertheless, it was then that Dietl and his partner, Tommy Colleran, began rousting addicts, car strippers, burglars, fences, prostitutes and numbers runners for information. They barged into smoke shops, after-hours bars and numbers joints. Against the rules and regulations, they dipped into the underworld for help and got a tip from an outraged organized crime chief they knew from the area.

It was the kind of street-wise police work that works. Within three days, Dietl and Colleran had the two rapists. Awards, plaques, letters from politicians, and newspaper and TV stories poured in on Dietl and Colleran. The brass at headquarters, reluctantly forced to promote him to the detective division, chose to bury him in an impoverished section of Brooklyn, where he helped get the Palm Sunday Killer.

Obviously, Dietl should have been the kind of cop any department would want to keep, but he was also a traditional cop. He didn't fit the new computerized-cop mold. So, when he turned in his shield and papers, there was no effort on the part of the department to keep him. There was also no attempt to thank or reward him for his service. As far as the brass was concerned, the less Dietl had to say, the better.

But now it's Dietl's turn and with his common sense and street savvy, he tells us more about our impotence in fighting crime than all the doctoral theses being studied by desk-bound cops looking for their paper promotions.

Nicholas Pileggi
New York, 1988

Chapter 1

October 10, 1981

Ordinarily, you get blown down by the noise of a live stationhouse. Cops are just naturally loud. They walk like elephants, they bang things around, they yell instead of talk. It's the kind of place, if you wanna be heard, you gotta speak up. It's not like walking into a library.

So I was a little surprised when I didn't hear the usual uproar when I came to work that night. I never knew that silence could be so loud.

I was doing decoys out of the Two Five Precinct in East Harlem. This is a Saturday, which is my busy season. All the muggers will be out shopping for victims. My head is getting set like cement for sitting in some pissy doorway waiting for someone to attack me, which is what decoy duty is all about.

Then I walk into this, this . . . I don't know what to make of it. Usually, you can hear the bitching a mile away. Especially on a Saturday. Prisoners are bitching about getting busted. Civilians are bitching about politicians and landlords. Cops are bitching about all the bitching.

But not tonight. None of the sergeants were yelling for coffee. The prisoners were actually meek. The cops were quiet.

It was like walking into a tomb.

Bo Dietl, a veteran plainclothes police officer, made an educated guess. A cop's been shot. Nothing else could explain the reverential hush.

"What's going on?" he asked one of the pale detectives.

The detective hesitated, weighing whether or not to answer. Then he remembered that Bo was a cop, a member of the family, and replied:

"They raped a nun."

I know that I felt my knees get soft. It was a blow. No doubt about it. Some things you don't expect. Even if you've seen everything. Even if you're made of stone. Even if you expect it.

I was shocked. Then I thought what everybody thought:

Nothing is sacred.

"From the convent?" asked Bo.

The detective nodded. "They raped her inside."

Our Lady of Mount Carmel Convent stood like an unsteady high-wire walker on 116th Street and an avenue called Pleasant. It teetered on the line where the last defiant Italians waited to be pushed into the suburbs by the approaching blacks and Hispanics.

The holdouts accepted the inevitability of their dislocation with a mixture of fatalism and rage. One by one, the outposts fell. And the small flock of nuns who lived in such open innocence among them were like symbols of their own vulnerability.

"Inside the convent?" asked Bo.

"Inside," replied the detective.

Not that they hadn't all feared just that. Not that they hadn't been listening with some third ear for that bulletin, for that social rumble that would signal a final shifting of the ground.

Bo and his partner, Detective Tommy Colleran (known for sufficient cause as "Cowboy"), jumped into their unmarked cruiser and ran the lights to the brick convent. It was ten blocks, and Bo turned on the siren and smacked the magnetic dome light on the roof as if he were on a hot run, as if there were still some chance to save the nun.

At the convent, the police cars with their flashing lights were scattered like rage. A street full of blinking fists.

It was grim. Not one break in the action. You know, one of the things cops do, we have a very soothing influence on a crime scene. Someone's in charge. You can relax. It's safe. But not here. The tension was still very high. Here, it's like we were the victims.

Bo spotted an old friend, Pete Christianson, taking charge. They had gone through the Police Academy together more than a decade ago. Their careers had taken different turns, but going through the academy together remains an old school tie. Now Christianson was a detective working in the Manhattan Sex Crimes

Unit, already, planting the flag of the unit over the case.

Everybody wants a big case. It's not just the action, although that counts for something. Big rewards go with big cases. Promotions. Recognition. Naturally, you're gonna get a lot of ugly little backdoor fights over who runs the investigation. Major Case Squad wants a piece. Borough Detectives wants it. Sex Crimes says it's theirs. There's a lot of nasty competition and politics and jealousy when it comes down to who gets the big jobs.

And it's right from the first because catching the case is already half the glory.

"Petey, what happened?" asked Bo.

Detective Christianson shook his head. "It's crazy, Bo."

Bo Dietl was no threat. Just a plainclothes precinct cop, not one of the prowling downtown hotshots looking to steal a big case. Christianson pointed across the street at the beige sandstone building that housed the convent. "Two guys. They went in! They actually went inside and raped a nun!"

The policemen stood across the street and looked at the convent, squinted, then turned away. "A thirty-year-old nun," continued Christianson. "A little thing you could hold in one hand."

And he held out his upturned hand, as if he could actually hold the little nun in his palm. Then his voice became brittle. "They punched the shit out of her. They raped her. They sodomized her. . . ."

You listen to the details of crimes over the years and you get a little hard. It doesn't mean so much after

4

you've seen it fifty, a hundred times. It becomes, like, you know, the words that you put into a report. "Perpetrator then proceeded to force the alleged victim to perform various acts of sodomy including . . ."
But this was different. This was a nun.

"They stuck a broom in her," said Christianson. "They actually stuck a broom in her. Then they stuck candles in her. It's hard to believe. They carved crosses all over her butt. And on her breasts. Twenty-seven crosses."

Who counted? A doctor. Not a cop. A cop would have covered her up. Been ashamed. Had to be a doctor to count the twenty-seven crosses carved on her behind and her breasts. A cop could not do it.

The number 27 gave the story ballast. It was a police detail. Not a wild rumor. Not an emotional figment. Corroboration. Substance. Counted crosses. An official detail.

"They used a sharpened nail file. We found it. There was blood on the nail file. They may even have used a crucifix. We're still checking. Maybe one of the crosses in the convent is missing.

"Then they pissed on her. Pissed on her and threw her down a flight of stairs and left her for dead."

Tommy Colleran groaned. "Oh, Mother of God. Oh, no!" He was pounding himself on the chest. "They didn't do that!" he wailed.

The police were not at their professional best. Every once in a while, a cop would stop what he was doing—checking the street for debris, looking for fingerprints, interviewing a bystander—and just stand frozen in the glare of oncoming implications.

"How is she?" asked Bo.

"Who?" said Christianson, startled by such a direct question. Most of the cops had just listened and made comments or uttered oaths.

"The nun," pressed Bo. "How is she?"

"How do you think?"

"She's not dead?"

"No, she's not dead. She's in shock."

So was everyone else. Dazed detectives went through the motions of an investigation. Forensic and technical teams went in and out of the convent, faces sagging with defeat.

The uniformed men brought in for crowd control were unnecessary. The crowds were held back by revulsion. The civilians stood on far sidewalks and watched in pinched fear. They thought what the cops thought: Nothing is sacred.

Detectives and plainclothes teams circled the building looking for something. A discarded weapon. A bloody piece of clothing. A telltale something.

The questioning of the bystanders followed the normal routine. Did you see someone? Who comes here on Saturday? Was there a stranger?

The detectives working in East Harlem were like most New York City police detectives—second- and third-generation Irish and Italians; former choirboys out of Queens and Brooklyn with an indelible trace of Catholic awe. They expected sin—it was part of man's flawed nature. But there were still taboos, unthinkable crimes that ran like a shiver through their ranks.

Inevitably, they had come to fear for the inhabitants of the convent. It became a routine, as they passed the convent on their rounds, to utter admonitions like prayers. Be careful, Sister. Be sure to lock the doors! Watch where you go. Walk near the gutter. God bless!

They knew something that the nuns didn't know: in the Two Five, unthinkable crimes were recorded daily on the precinct blotter.

The gentle nuns smiled indulgently, humoring the nice policemen, convinced, as their faith decreed, that they were exempt from all secular consequences.

The policemen took no comfort in the fact that they'd been right.

While Petey is talking to me and Tommy is pounding his chest, I am looking at the convent. Studying it. This is a crime. There's somebody who did it. That's our business. You gotta be a professional.

Bo Dietl was regarded as a flamboyant showboat by most members of the NYPD. His media-prone nature was considered pure vanity.

But there was no denying his talent. In the turmoil of a crisis, he became—always—a cop. He was clear-eyed and had a commonsense knack for seeing the connecting dots that completed a picture. He had something else that, like his explosive personality, would not be weighed in his favor when it came time to advance his career: he had a true sixth sense.

The book cops who ran the department along technical lines would never acknowledge it, they would never credit it as a valid credential, but it was there all the same. Everyone who ever worked with Bo Dietl had seen it in action.

"This doesn't look like a sex crime to me," he said, standing across the street, looking at the brownstone next door to the convent. The roof of the four-story apartment house led down to the roof of the three-story convent like a step. "This looks to me like a burglary. It turned into a sex crime, but it started out as a burglary."

Christianson bristled. "This is a sex crime," he said with utter finality. "End of story."

Technically, they were peers, but he had just tried to shove Bo off the case.

Already the bolstering teams of veteran detectives were arriving in their unmistakable unmarked cars. From all the high commands in the city, the picked detectives with their gleaming first-grade gold shields were assembling. They all had their retinues and their reputations.

Bo didn't stand a chance. He was a thirty-year-old plainclothes cop with a silver shield and a bad reputation with the superchiefs. He might have accumulated the greatest arrest record in the history of decoy work, he might have sat through a thousand nights of undercover, but he was overdue for promotion because of his antic ways. He was quick-tempered and vaguely impudent.

The bad-boy style might be overlooked—after all, a lot of good cops liked to drink and stay out late and raise hell—but there was a very disturbing quality of independence that they detected in Bo Dietl. He seemed to live by his own, private code of honor. Not by the fifteen hundred explicit pages of the department rules and regulations.

Bo wrote his own guidelines. If he was taunted into a fight by some street tough, he would settle it man to man. He wouldn't add on charges afterward.

And he wouldn't use his gun. In one confrontation, when he was facing down a madman armed with a knife—while a lieutenant stood across the street and ordered him to shoot—Bo talked to the man, fooled him, and tackled him, without firing his weapon. He did get cut, but he didn't have to kill the man.

There was something that outweighed everything else. Something about Bo Dietl frightened them. It was his strength. He was just short of five-feet-eight, but he had incredible physical power. He could lift cars with his bare hands. After a night of drinking, he could wrench parking meters out of the cement. And he was the arm-wrestling champion of the entire police department.

For some reason, this troubled the men who ran the police department. It was as if they didn't quite have him under control. They could take away his shield and his gun, but they couldn't take away his strength. It was as if Bo Dietl had a secret, unlicensed weapon. Which is pretty much how Bo felt about it.

"This is not your case," said Petey Christianson.

Yeah, okay, I get the hint. But I had an inkling about this one. Something in my scalp. Me and Tommy hang around long enough to pick up whatever we can pick up and then we get out of there. But I have a feeling.

9

Chapter 2

The corner bar at 119th Street and Park Avenue in upper Manhattan had perfect protection. Just down the street was the Twenty-fifth Police Precinct.

The officers assigned to the stationhouse had adopted the back room of the bar as their unofficial headquarters. There were always cops going on or off duty playing poker on the scratchy tables of the back room. In addition to the endless poker game, there were always gossip and company in the clubby comforts of the bar. After a long night of poker and companionship, cops would emerge blinking in the unexpected daylight.

The special teams assigned to crack the rape of the nun became a fixture in the back room as well. Like the others, they were there to blow off steam. They unstrung their neckties and gambled and dulled their painful work with the usual blunt instrument: whiskey.

The initial rage had turned into the professional grind of following threads. Because of the nature of the crime, there was a charged atmosphere, a sense of high purpose among the teams.

Apart from the pressures of duty and conscience, the investigators heard a clock ticking. So far, they had kept the story out of the newspapers and off the air. The streets would have been overrun with camera crews throwing the fear of the five o'clock news into nervous witnesses. Reporters would have camped like assassins outside of the convent. Once the story was loose, it would shut down any possibility of discretion. Or dignity.

But the cops had been lucky. The media, with their Balkanized view of Manhattan, hadn't caught on. Anything that happened above Ninety-sixth Street was regarded as foreign news, outside of the range of the prime yuppie markets. The media didn't cover Spanish Harlem with the same zest that they did, say, a restaurant opening in midtown. But sooner or later, they were bound to hear about it. The rape of a nun had too many tabloid possibilities to remain undiscovered for long. Already rumors were trickling downtown, protected from assignment editors by their sheer implausibility.

The elite detectives were systematically going house to house, door to door. Cross-checking neighbors, using classic, textbook routine. Comb the ground, assemble all the pieces. Read and reread the reports. Sometimes you see things in the light of some fresh, second sight. Reinterview witnesses. People unwilling or confused or in the opening stages of shock often remembered details later.

Watching all this, with his own impatient clock, was

Bo Dietl. He was not among the elect working on the case, and it was a painful exclusion. Bo, like a green plant, had a natural inclination toward the limelight.

However, he had a more urgent problem. His partner. Tommy Colleran was suffering badly. Tommy was drinking hard liquor like a man dying of thirst. One right after the other. "Take it easy, partner," said Bo, looking over from the poker table.

Tommy nodded and kept on drinking.

It wasn't only the nun, although Tommy was an old-fashioned Catholic who took it hard. What emptied the liquor bottles on those quick nights in October were the parking tickets.

"Pay attention to the cards," said one of the players to Bo.

Bo had trouble concentrating. His partner's career was in jeopardy and the reason was incomprehensibly stupid. The seemingly trivial nature of it almost made matters worse. Tommy Colleran, holder of a chestful of decorations including one of the police department's highest awards for bravery, was about to be undone by a thicket of parking tickets.

He had a job-related excuse, but no one was buying it. An ardent family man, Tommy lived on Sixty-sixth Street and First Avenue with his wife and five kids. Anti-crime assignments ate up days whole, which was a hardship for a strong family man. So, whenever Tommy had off time, he went home. He parked where he could, and usually, the spots were illegal.

Not even the old card planted in the window from the Patrolmen's Benevolent Association, identifying Tommy as a cop, helped. The traffic enforcement agents were out to prove that they were incorruptible. It was a hard season for careless parkers.

Tommy shoveled the tickets into his glove compartment where they remained, forgotten and unpaid.

The wicked scandals of New York City's high municipal officials had not yet surfaced and so the appetite of the city's newspapers for corruption had to be satisfied with parking violators. They printed long lists of outstanding scofflaws. Especially scofflaws on the public payroll. Tommy Colleran's name appeared on the list of major traffic scofflaws. A full-throated outcry ensued. The departmental bluestockings found it intolerable that an active detective should disgrace the police department by ignoring parking tickets. Internal Affairs began an investigation. There was talk of a trial board, a threat to take away Tommy's gold shield.

They would make of him an example.

If Tommy Colleran was threatened, so was Bo Dietl. They were partners.

Partnerships among police are always intense, but in an anti-crime unit the tangle of bonds and obligations and affection are jungle thick.

In 1977, when Bo returned to the anti-crime unit and was asked to go back out on decoy duty—the most dangerous assignment in police work—he agreed on condition that he could handpick his backup.

Choosing a backup was anything but casual. A backup had to be tough and reliable and possess some protective instincts that would reassure in some inexpressible way the exposed partner. A backup was all that stood between the decoy and an inspector's funeral.

Bo approached Tommy Colleran and Jack Freck,

who was a third partner in the anti-crime team, to see if they could become partners. Before they even met, Bo knew about Tommy's reputation—and his eccentricity. Tommy thought that he was John Wayne. Once, facing an armed bandit, Tommy had just smiled thinly, the way the Duke might, and said in that soft, rolling John Wayne voice: "Okay, Pilgrim, straight up or over the saddle; makes no difference to me." The gunman was rocked by the wild, icy nerve of the cop and surrendered without putting up a fight.

He had heard about Tommy as he sat at the bar, the way they used to sit around campfires. Bo learned how Tommy had come to be called Cowboy. They said that Tommy kept a running tally of the number of times someone took a shot at him. It was up to twenty-two. And they hadn't all missed. Cowboy was off duty when he got into a fight in a strange bar a few years back with some civilian. They stepped outside to settle it and Tommy, obeying the code of the West, left his gun behind. Trouble was that the civilian was an easterner and promptly emptied his own illegal pistol into Cowboy.

Cowboy was shot up pretty bad, but he didn't want his wife to know just how bad. In all, there were five bullets scattered around his body. When Cowboy's wife showed up in the emergency room, Tommy had a twisted smile on his face and kept saying, "Now, now, it ain't really that bad." His wife sympathetically touched his shoulder and Tommy winced. "Oh, uh, careful, honey, I stopped a little lead there." Rattled, his wife took his hand. "Uh, I caught some lead there, too." She was shaken. She sat down and her hand fell on Tommy's thigh. Again he flinched. "Not there, either, little lady."

"Where can I touch you?" she cried.
Cowboy pointed out the lead-free zones.

Bo and Cowboy hit it off at once. They had unspoken areas of agreement. Tommy knew Bo's legend and Bo knew Tommy's. During the first interview, when they were circling each other in a kind of professional courtship, deciding whether or not they would fit together, Tommy talked about himself.

"I killed a man over on Park Avenue," he said, his creased face like stone, looking around the room the way a gunfighter might keep track of his environment. "It was under the railroad there. You know the spot. He opened up on me, point-blank. Had to kill him. No choice."

Bo just sat there, listening. He knew that boasting about gunplay wasn't the point of the story.

"He was just a kid," said Cowboy. "Well, you kill a kid, even if he's nineteen or twenty, he's still a kid. Even if he's shooting at you. It's got to bother you. Bothered me. I couldn't sleep. I had nightmares. So, finally, I went to see the mother. She invited me in and she sat me down on the couch. I told her that I was sorry I had to kill her son and she said that it was all right. She said she understood. She said that I saved a lot of innocent people from a lot of misery."

Cowboy looked over at Bo, then looked away. "Well, I got real angry. I left there and I'm telling you I was hot. I mean, slap my face, scream at me, get mad, do something. But don't thank me for killing your son!"

Bo, who could not even bring himself to draw his gun on a man attacking him with a knife, understood. This was a man who would not be careless with a life. This was a man he could trust.

"There's just one question I have to ask you," said Bo. "If I get killed, you have to promise me that you'll get the guy who kills me."

Tommy said, "You got it, partner."

Bo could relax.

At bottom, going out on decoy required more than simple bravery. It required vast faith. No one could endure the misery of nights curled up in frozen puddles of urine waiting to be mugged without some belief. The belief itself could vary. It could be a belief in social order or a religious belief. Bo had to believe that his death would not be in vain, that he would be avenged. Tommy Colleran was his afterlife.

As it turned out, it was a famous partnership, The Pit Bull and the Cowboy. Bo was small and vivid. Tommy was tall and had that slow swagger. Bo had a wild, windblown streak; he was a happy brawler. Cowboy was a quiet accomplice, as if he were secretly amused by his partner's stunts. He was twelve years older than Bo, but that was fine. Bo always required some older, more mature hand to restrain his rampant enthusiasm.

Bo was worried about Cowboy, but Cowboy wasn't the only member of the team in hot water. Bo was being investigated on a charge all too common in his record: brutality.

The problem was Bo's size. He was short. And there was also that baby face. Criminals and tough guys tended to underestimate him. They'd pull away when he took their arm to make an arrest. They'd take a swing. And before they even knew what hit them, Bo would turn off their lights. He never started it, but he didn't exactly run away from a fistfight, either. In fact, the truth is that he enjoyed it. He took his share of punishment—he left his nose out on the street—but there was satisfaction in summary punishment. So Bo Dietl, the Pit Bull, was always answering this kind of charge:

It was two drug dealers. I busted them during the summer. Late one night. They came at me. I don't know where Cowboy was, maybe he was off that night. They came at me and we're rolling around in the gutter and I guess I broke a few of their bones. Happens in a fight. They were trying to kill me. No doubt. It was hairy. These are serious drug dealers.

Somebody called Nine One One and told them a cop is getting killed out on 135th Street. They know I'm a cop because I'm a white guy. All of a sudden, everybody's showing up. You hear a ten-thirteen and you go. That's a cop in trouble. That's one thing about the Two Five. They just went when they got a ten-thirteen. Guys showed up with food in their mouths.

So then these two drug dealers file a civilian complaint, of which I have several—none ever confirmed. But, you know, people think, where there's smoke, right?

The district attorney decides to take the case before a grand jury. The DAs do not like me anyway. I have put a few of their noses out of joint, so they don't mind bringing me before a grand jury. No love lost. That Wednesday—this is four days after the rape—I have to appear.

Well, the grand jury listens to the drug dealers and they listen to me and then my lawyer plays the Nine One One tapes. That's all they had to hear. There were a couple of calls. Not just one. They all said that a couple of guys are going to kill this bearded white guy. I'm the bearded white guy. They all confirmed that I'm

17

*the one being attacked. The grand jury listens to the
tapes, and the district attorney is lucky they do not
indict him.*

As he emerged from the grand jury on Centre Street
in lower Manhattan on that Wednesday afternoon, Bo
Dietl passed a newsstand. The afternoon tabloid had a
huge banner headline. One of their screamers. It was
the story of a nun being raped in East Harlem.

Chapter 3

"What are you doing about it?"

Bo threw up his hands. "What do you want from me, Felix?"

"I want to know what you are doing about it," persisted Felix Brinkman in that clipped German accent that he had brought over with him from Europe thirty years earlier. His hand grasped Bo's shoulder like a claw.

"Hey, I'm not Superman," said Bo, pulling away. "It's not even my case."

Felix started banging glasses. Pushing them down the counter to the bartender, stating his objections in the clash of crystal. The news about the outrage was out and had quickly become the latest watershed marker to measure the plunge of civilization. At Adam's Apple, the singles bar on First Avenue and Sixty-first Street, the young secretaries and executive trainees and the investment bankers and legal assistants used the case as one more proof of the society's inevitable decline, one more sigh of despair, one more excuse for quick cohabitation.

Felix, however, a part owner of the bar, was not going to take it lying down. He might look like a withered old toothpick, but he was still a battler and he knew that Bo worked in the precinct where the rape had occurred. As he saw it, it was his job to get Bo off his backside so that he could crack the case.

"If anybody can do anything . . . ," hissed Felix into Bo's ear. He left the rest unsaid.

"You made your point, Felix. Go check some IDs."

Felix was Bo's greatest fan and Adam's Apple had become Bo's chief midtown hangout. Bo scattered hangouts around town like a sailor setting up house in different ports. But Adam's Apple was his favorite. The men were interesting and the women were pretty and the drinks were free. Felix, who liked having a cop around, would never let him pick up a tab.

Bo had to smile at the old man's persistence. Felix was like a snapping dog, he thought. But then, you had to be ferocious to survive the Holocaust. Felix had earned the mean streak, as well as the twisted sense of humor. Once, at a Halloween party, Felix Brinkman came dressed as a Nazi storm trooper. And he laughed at the shock from customers with more dainty sensibilities. But he was a victim of the SS and he had a right to wear any old chip on his shoulder.

This was Bo's kind of guy.

Felix took a huge vicarious interest in Bo's career. After a night on decoy, Bo would come into the bar and unwind, telling Felix all the lurid details of his work. Bo needed to talk and Felix needed to listen. While the patrons went through the usual stammering of modern social small talk, Bo and Felix would sit for hours at a corner table, both listening to the music of

Bo's stories. Bo said that talking to Felix was like talking to his son.

If it seemed, on the surface, a bizarre friendship—the daredevil young cop and the screwball bar owner—there were deeper things that they had in common. Crazy courage, for example. One night, when three young halfbacks had had too much to drink and began bothering some of the women, Bo had to step in. Politely, he asked the men to take it easy, to quit pestering the customers. But they were in no mood for conciliation and a brawl broke out. As Bo was trading punches with a couple of the heavyweights, he noticed Felix out of the corner of his eye, another pit bull, pounding away at the third guy. His opponent was three times younger and twice his size, but it didn't stop Felix.

Bo admired that kind of gumption. That, and Felix's unflagging enthusiasm. Bo liked having his own troubadour. It wasn't long before he took Felix out on decoys so that he could watch him being robbed, so that he would have firsthand material about his idol.

Felix knew that Bo was tough, but being invited to watch his friend being mugged was an honor. It deepened his admiration, as well as providing some eyewitness thrills. He saw the young cop take on two men with knives. Before the backups could jump in, Bo was rolling around in the gutter with the thieves. And, Felix noted, he was enjoying it!

But that was all prologue now. Felix could not put aside thoughts of the nun rape.

"This is important," he persisted.

"I know."

"This is the most important case in the history of New York."

"You're getting carried away," replied Bo, ordering another glass of liquor.

They sat there for a moment and then Bo emptied his glass, looked over at Felix's miserable expression, and made up his mind. He leaned over and whispered his decision.

"I'm gonna break this case," he told Felix.

The old man's eyes lit up. He slammed his hands on the table.

"That's it!" said Felix. "Now I know it's gonna be solved. Now I know!"

"Shhh!" said Bo, looking around, checking to see if there were any other cops in the room. "You gotta be quiet about this." Felix was bobbing his head like a child. "It's not my case," explained Bo. "I'm not even supposed to work on it."

"But you will?" asked Felix.

"I will," said Bo.

"It's as good as solved," said Felix, getting up and doing a little dance.

Felix was not the only one putting pressure on Bo to jump into the nun investigation. There were his buddies from the bar at the Doral Hotel, professional ball players and gamblers and night owls who sat around ragging Bo, asking what the hotshot cop from the Two Five was doing to bring in the creeps who raped a nun in his own backyard. Bo was not happy about being teased.

It was not the same thing as the pleas from Felix. Felix was a fan. When everyone else went home, he'd still be there. But now Bo was starting to catch it from a larger audience. Men he had to work to impress.

Jimmy Weston owned a restaurant on Fifty-fourth Street between Lexington and Park avenues. He kept a rough scorecard of Bo's career and now he was growing impatient. What's going on, Bo? Why haven't you caught these guys?

It was embarrassing.

"I can't talk about it," said Bo through the clenched teeth of his own frustration.

Then there were the "Italian businessmen" up in East Harlem. These were the local Mafia chiefs with long Catholic memories who were still capable of being scandalized. Known members of organized crime, who would one day have to answer for a lot of bodies dumped in empty lots, offered a reward for the capture of the rapists, dead or alive. And it was clear which of the two conditions they preferred. They declared a temporary truce with the police department—the way Lucky Luciano did during World War II when he went from a New York State prison to Sicily to settle a labor strike to help the war effort. The "hard" mob guys became lambs, turning over leads and giving up squealers for the sake of bringing in the culprits.

At the Colonial Bar he ran into Fish, Sammy and Fat Tony, who all pressed, with that nasty smile. What are you doing about the nun case?

Bo couldn't go anyplace. Every store owner, every housewife, every kid in the street—that's all they talked about. Bo felt as if he had personally let everyone down. He was the symbol of the police and he was not doing anything about the great outrage.

When Bo Dietl showed up for a veal sandwich at one of the fine Italian restaurants in East Harlem, a CEO from a major crime family was waiting to speak to him. "We trust you, Bo," said the Mafia chief. This was not idle flattery. Bo had grown up in a section of Queens thick with Italian mobsters. His friends in school had been the sons of high Mafia officers. The word among New York City's crime families was that Bo Dietl was "good people." No letter of credit carried more weight.

The "businessman" was sitting at a table with his back to the wall. Two bodyguards hovered nearby. Bo sat across the table. "We trust you and we hope that you can do something about this terrible crime."

"I appreciate that," replied Bo carefully. "That's very kind of you. Naturally, we're all doing what we can."

He always showed respect to the Mafia chiefs, who were like oriental overlords when it came to their dignity. Then the Mafia chief said something that was bound to touch Bo's weakness:

"We know that we can count on you, Bo. We know what kind of man you are."

Bo lost his appetite. He left the restaurant and returned to the corner bar—the police hangout. He couldn't even confide in Tommy. His partner was going down for the third time inside a bottle of Scotch whiskey.

All night long, they sat in the bar. Bo ordered a plate of food for Tommy, but it lay untouched on the counter.

"It's not the end of the world," he told Tommy, and Tommy looked at him with his puffy, bleary eyes. It was the end of his world. A bunch of parking tickets was going to cost him his career.

Nine days after the rape, Bo was having dinner at Rao's, the famous Italian restaurant where celebrities came to dine in East Harlem, when Vinnie Rao, the owner, pulled him into the kitchen.

"I hear the people who did this are from One Hundred and Twenty-fifth Street," he told Bo.

24

"Yeah?" said Bo.

Vinnie Rao pulled Bo even closer, making certain no one overheard.

"I hear it pretty good."

"Thanks, Vinnie, I appreciate this."

"A Hundred Twenty-fifth Street. You find those bastards."

"I'm doing my best, Vinnie," said Bo, who wasn't even working on the case.

By the eleventh day, no one was showing any progress. The files were barren of clues. There were hundreds of phone calls—someone saw someone suspicious, someone hated their husband—but all without foundation, all sand.

The elite units were getting a little testy. The citizens were throwing nasty comments at cops. How come you hassle drivers when you should be out catching the person who raped the nun?

The whole town was in a bad mood. Bo called Pete Christianson in the Sex Crimes Unit.

"Pete, level with me. Do you guys have anything?"

"Nothing, Bo. It's a fucking desert. We are pissing in the wind."

"Well, I heard from one of my people that they come from One Twenty-fifth Street."

"Oh, yeah? You heard that? We heard that, too."

"You did?" said Bo, getting a little excited, thinking maybe he had a hand in this one after all.

"And we heard One Sixteenth Street. And Ninety-sixth Street. And Plattsburgh. Listen, Bo: all we hear are bullshit tips. We got a hundred fifty, two hundred locations. This don't tell me shit."

"I get the idea."

"But don't hesitate to call, pal. We need all the help we can get."

"Right."

But for some reason, the 125th Street tip sounded right to Bo. He had no reason to believe it, beyond that inexplicable itch of premonition. He had done his duty. He had called Christianson to pass it along—he didn't want to blow an ongoing investigation. If they were closing in on someone, Pete would have warned him to back off. But it was clear that the field was wide open. Christianson did everything but laugh out loud at the tip. Bo Dietl decided to make his move. He went into the captain's office in the Twenty-fifth Precinct stationhouse and shut the door behind him. The captain started congratulating Bo for his and Tommy's work on a couple of big cases that they had broken—a string of thirty Chinese robberies and a homicide.

"Thanks, Captain. I want some time."

"What for?"

"To work on the nun case."

"You know that case belongs to Sex Crimes."

"I know. But it's not a sex crime."

"It sure sounds like one. Rape, sodomy. I call that a sex crime."

"Doesn't make sense, Captain. We know there were two guys. You ever hear of two guys working as a team to go out on a sex crime?"

The captain's face wrinkled in a disturbing thought.

"It was a burglary team," pressed Bo. "The sex was an afterthought."

The captain knew that Bo had a point, but he also understood the departmental pecking order, the political problems that would occur when units stepped on the toes of other units already in the field. Cops could be as touchy as women who show up at a party wearing the same dress. "It's assigned to Sex Crimes," he said, ducking the question.

"I'm looking for the people who raped the nun, Captain."

"So are a lot of other cops. You already have a job," said the captain, going back to his paperwork.

Bo stood there.

"All right," said the captain, leaning back in his chair, "let's hear it. What have you got?"

"I got a feeling," said Bo.

The captain waited. No more was coming.

"That's it? A feeling?"

"It's a strong feeling."

"You expect me to pull you off the chart because you got a feeling?"

"I never had such a strong feeling before, Captain."

"I got a feeling you're jerking me off."

"Captain, I'm telling you, this is a very strong feeling. And I heard some things."

"You heard some things? Did you pass these things along?"

"I called my pal Pete Christianson and he said they were up to their ass in alligators. He wasn't interested. But, Captain, I'm telling you, I got this feeling."

They faced each other for a long time. Finally, the captain said crisply: "Okay, three days."

"Thanks, Cap," said Bo.

"No more."

"No more."

"Saturday, you're back on the clock."

Tommy was at his regular post, standing at the bar, looking a little unsteady. Bo started drinking with him. Two hours later, he broke the news.

"We're off the chart, partner," said Bo.

"Rrrright," said Cowboy. "Trouble at the ranch because I double-parked my horse."

"We're working the nun case."

Tommy straightened. His eyes focused.

"You have something?" he asked soberly.

"I want you to go home and get some sleep. Take a shower and meet me back here at eight in the morning."

As Tommy started to leave, he stopped, turned, and looked at Bo.

"We're gonna be all right, partner," said Bo. "We'll break this fucking case and be heroes. Then they'll never take your shield."

Tommy left to clean up, to prepare. He walked away with his old cowboy gait.

Chapter 4

By Thursday, October 22, twelve days after the rape, the shock had shifted into anger and the brute fact had sunk in. The people of New York smoldered. It came out in many forms. There were official expressions, such as that of Mayor Edward I. Koch, who called the rape a "despicable act of depravity" and announced a ten-thousand-dollar reward for the apprehension of the villains.

And there were unlikely cries for justice that came from improbable quarters. The "wise guys"—men connected to organized crime families—who grew up in the area and now returned from plush suburbs to conduct street-corner transactions in the usual trades—loan sharking and gambling—offered a cash bounty for the heads of the rapists. It was a "contract" without mercy. Word was passed on the street that twenty-five thousand dollars would be paid for the deaths of the rapists. No one disagreed with the mobster who confidently predicted: "They will die within a month."

There were also polite outbursts of public fury. The *New York Daily News* seemed to capture a terrifying possibility, namely that events were out of control. "As horrifying as the crime itself, however, is what it seems to say about life in this city. This act of perverted cruelty against a holy sister is bound to make a lot of people wonder if New York City is somehow near the end, with no one and no place safe any more."

Sister Yolanda De Mola, one of the leaders of the Sisters of Charity, the order housed at the convent, wrote an open letter to the rapists. "Where has society failed you that your rage and impotence could take such a form? I am appalled by your actions. . . ."

In a guarded room of Saint Vincent's Hospital, far away from the scene of the crime, the bruised and mutilated nun was unable to describe her attackers. She told the police that she had been on her way up to the roof at ten-thirty in the morning to check on a noise. The door of the roof was ajar because there had been workmen on the roof. On the third-floor landing, she was seized, but she couldn't say by whom. There were two of them, she thought. She could not be certain.

But the attack was still too fresh in her mind. They ripped off her clothing. They were frenzied, wild. One held her down and committed the sexual violations while the other went to work with the nail file. They tortured her for an hour and a half.

She was beyond shock. Beyond comprehension. She did not grasp what had happened to her. She worked in the school. She taught children. She was a teaching nun. This was . . . she did not know what.

Meanwhile, in the East Harlem precinct that had been taken over as the headquarters for the investigation, the cream of the city's three thousand detectives assembled for the manhunt. Everyone seemed to want a piece of the action. There were Transit Authority detectives as well as Housing Authority detectives in the bay. There were squads from the Manhattan Homicide Task Force, as well as investigators from the Bias Squad.

The spread of talent was supposed to provide a collegial pool of investigators. But it didn't. It just became a bazaar of jealous competition.

Hundreds of detectives ran in all directions. There was no single command, no one in charge. There were loud briefings and high-pitched conversations that gave the squad room an atmosphere of hysteria.

Bo Dietl stood at the door of the squad room, watching, amused.

It looked like a lot of chickens running around without heads. I never saw so many bosses. All chiefs and very few Indians. And you know what? These guys didn't know what they were doing. They were strangers in the area. They didn't even know where to go to get a cup of coffee. There may have been some great detectives up there, but they didn't know the first thing about the neighborhood. These streets belonged to me. They were my people out there. I knew when I looked at that, that we had a shot.

In a corner of the room, trying to keep out of the way, was Cowboy. He was scrubbed, shaved, and rested. He'd had only a few hours of sleep, but it was enough. He was drinking coffee and running on the high octane of revived hope.

"Hey, partner!" he said brightly as Bo came into the squad room on that morning.

They were both grinning as if they had already cracked the case.

"You okay?" asked Bo.

"You're looking at one healthy scofflaw."

"We got until Saturday," said Bo.

"Sounds about right," said Cowboy.

"Maybe Sunday." They were trying to stay out of earshot of the other detectives.

Cowboy asked a question that had been bothering him all night. "What exactly have we got?"

Bo smiled. "Nothing."

"Nothing?"

"Unless you count a feeling."

"You got me all hot over a fuckin' hunch?"

"It's a powerful hunch, partner."

"It better be a burning bush."

But Bo was smiling and Cowboy suspected something more than a whim. Cowboy had seen Bo's hunches work before.

"A little more than a hunch; Vinnie Rao said that these guys come from One Hundred and Twenty-fifth Street," said Bo.

"You heard that?"

"From Vinnie Rao."

"Are we whistling through our asshole, partner, or is this a solid lead?"

"He seemed pretty sure."

"You will forgive me, but this sounds a little thin to me."

"If it was easy, the pussies from Sex Crimes would have solved it."

"True."

"Relax. We also got a description. One short. One tall. Mutt and Jeff. One guy limps. And they're from One Hundred and Sixteenth Street."

"That's it?"

"We got as good a shot as anyone. C'mon, let's go park illegally," said Bo.

They began where all investigations begin: the scene of the crime. They drove over to Pleasant Avenue and stood across the street and looked at the convent from this new angle—working detectives.

"See the ladder?" said Bo.

A fire escape ran like an invitation from the roof of the adjoining brownstone to the roof of the convent.

"That's how they got in," said Bo.

Cowboy stared, imagining two men climbing down the ladder onto the roof.

"Easiest way to break in," said Cowboy.

"That's how they did it," said Bo with complete certainty. "Couple of junkies."

"Junkies?"

"Nobody else but a degenerate junkie is gonna break into a convent," said Bo. "Nobody with a full deck thinks they can get away with it. Gotta be a wild-ass desperado junkie to pull that kind of shit. Sex deviate comes in through the front door. He comes in alone. Burglars come in through the roof. Burglars come in pairs. Junkies go wild."

They circled the convent, Our Lady of Mount Carmel Church next door. They walked around the block, talked to some residents, fixed in their minds the layout of the area.

Then they went to 125th Street, where, according to Vinnie Rao, they would find the culprits.

One Hundred and Twenty-fifth street is the main artery that bisects Harlem. It runs from the academic fringes of Columbia University on the Hudson River on the West Side to the collapsing tenements on the East Side. By the time it hits the East River, with the Triborough Bridge that connects Manhattan to the suburbs, it runs out of hope.

There are hundreds of buildings along 125th Street, from projects to slums. When Vinnie Rao said that the people who raped the nun came from 125th Street, he could have meant that they lived there, or that they did business there, or that they came past there from time to time. Several hundred thousand people fell into the various categories.

Bo and Cowboy began with an apartment building on the eastern lip of the avenue, in the shadow of the bridge linking Manhattan to Queens and the Bronx. It was one of those crumbling walk-up tenements, with falling plaster and leaking plumbing and shaky stairs. Bo and Cowboy were two white men—unmistakably cops—going up and down the stairs like landlords trying to collect the rent. They knocked on doors that would not open.

"What do you want?" came a voice from inside. It was not a friendly voice. The door remained closed, and Bo and Cowboy had to shout through the reinforced locks.

"We're from the Two Five and we're working on a case," said Bo in his best, polite tone.

No sound came from the closed door. It was a statement.

"We're looking for a couple of guys—"

"I don't know no couple of guys."

And they could hear the feet padding away.

34

The reflex was understandable. There were doors that occasionally cracked open, and citizens peered out cautiously through the layers of chain locks.

"We're looking for two guys. One short. One tall. They're a burglary team. The short guy limps."

We were coming up negative. Everything was negative. Guys standing on the street watching us with little smiles because they knew we were striking out. The light was getting dim in my brain. But every time the light got dim, Tommy would see me getting depressed and say, "Come on, partner, let's go back out."

We skipped lunch and we skipped dinner and we just went door to door. It was brutal. Finally, it's ten o'clock at night and I said, "Let's call it quits." So we head over to the bar and we're having a few drinks. I mean, we figured it's all over, we put in all those hours, now we can relax and have a few drinks.

We have a couple of drinks, right. And all the guys are in there and all of a sudden Sergeant Stevens comes in. He's our anti-crime sergeant. And he says, "Where the fuck have you guys been all day? What is this, a roll-call special assignment, eight to four? What are you guys doing?"

So we tell him. And as we're talking, there's another detective listening. One of the regular detectives. And he's making fun of us. "Right, sure, working on the nun case. Yeah. Who the fuck are you kidding?" So Stevens turns around and he says, "Hey, go fuck yourself. These guys say they're working the nun case, they're working the nun case."

Stevens takes us aside. He says, "What have you got?" So I said, "I don't know what we got." I said, "I have this strong fucking feeling about One Hundred

*and Twenty-fifth Street." And the sarge smiles. He says,
"You know, Bo, you could fucking do it. I believe in you
guys."*

Which is all Bo ever really needed: someone to
believe in him. An audience.

Bo began to play some poker in the back room.
Killing time. The jokes rolled around the table, he
could feel the pinprick of ridicule, but somewhere
along the line, Bo felt his luck kick in. At two o'clock
in the morning he signaled to Tommy and they left the
bar.

They had been waiting for the pimps and hookers to
hit the street. The night was young. They stopped the
night shift, the pushers and pimps, the hookers and
homeless.

"We're looking for a couple of guys. Burglary
team."

"You're that crazy dude. Am I right?"

The pimp was smiling, looking at the business card
that Bo handed him. Bo was smiling, too. "That's me,
my man."

"You Bo, that dude that crashes through windows,
like Superman, am I right?"

"I have been known to make unusual entrances."

"Well, well, you are one famous dude."

"We're looking for a couple of guys. Burglars. One
short, one tall. The short one limps."

"You talkin' about black men?"

"I believe I am."

"I don't know anyone offhand."

"If you could keep an eye out and call us at this
number." Bo indicated the business card.

"Not only that, I will inform my staff."

The working girls giggled.

Bo and Cowboy passed out hundreds of such business cards along Park Avenue. Sometimes they watched them being torn up, tossed in the gutter, or crumpled with contempt. Bo and Cowboy had put in some time on this street. Some of these people did some time for them.

But often enough, they ran into people who respected them. Held no grudge. Promised to look out for a two-man Mutt-and-Jeff burglary team.

They hit them all, anyone with eyes to see and ears to listen. And they went all night long, back and forth, in case they missed someone.

Pretty soon I notice the sun coming up. We'd been going on coffee and sandwiches. So, I said to Tommy, "Let's quit." "No," he says. "We'll grab an hour in the car." And we did. A nap. One hour. Less. Then we went out and got a couple of beers to keep us going and we hit the street again. It was weird. Something drove us.

It was Friday.

The streets were dry by morning. There was a skeleton crew from the big-shot detective commands, but Bo noticed that they covered up the reports when he got close. They weren't going to share their clues with some vigilante anti-crime unit.

"One more time, partner," said Bo.

Back into the cruiser and up to 125th Street. They spotted a kid sitting on a television set in front of one of the tenements at the start of 125th Street.

"Did we hit that building?" asked Tommy.

"I think we skipped it," said Bo, getting out of the unmarked car.

Chapter 5

It's crazy. You go out and bust your tail and up comes nothing. You break regulations and talk to all the wise guys—because, let's face it, if you wanna know what's going down on the street, you gotta talk to the mob guys; they have the ears out there.

Technically, you're not supposed to talk to known criminals, which is stupid. Who are you supposed to talk to about crime, hairdressers? You gotta talk to known criminals! They know what's what, as far as crime goes. It's their business. They gotta keep up. But the regulations, which you can stick up your ass, say this is a violation. No talking to known criminals and no hanging out in bars or smoke shops or after-hours joints. Talk to good citizens and hang out in candy stores! The people who draw up these regulations are from the fucking moon. It's because they don't trust you. They think you're gonna be corrupted.

Well, I have never been one to let a stupid regulation

stand in the way of common sense. So you say fuck it and you go ahead and do your job because this is the only way it's gonna get done. You're not gonna find street gossip about second-story junkies in a fucking tea shop. You gotta hang out in nasty places and talk to the meanest fucks alive. You gotta hit all the drug locations and put the fear of God into them. "Man, it is going to get very bad up here. You are not going to put one needle in one arm until we get some help." Then you lay down the word of God to the pimps. "You are not going to have one single broad on the street until these guys are caught." Talk business. Get their attention.

But, it's crazy. All this shit, all this effort, all this sweat, and then you see a guy sitting on top of a television set, right out in plain sight on the sidewalk, like he's waiting for you.

"I know that guy," said Tommy, as they pulled up to the curb on 125th Street off Park Avenue.

"Yeah, he looks familiar to me, too."

"I think I locked him up once."

"Burglary, unless I miss my guess," joked Bo.

As they got out of the car, the young burglar tried to look innocent.

"Nice TV," said Bo.

"What TV?" said the burglar.

"The one that you're sitting on," said Bo.

"Oh," said the young burglar, shifting his weight, looking under him. "This TV."

"I bet I know what you're doing," said Bo. "You're waiting for an extension cord so you can watch the news, right?"

Tommy was quiet, waiting to play his part.

"Shit, this ain't my TV. I'm minding this for a friend," explained the burglar.

39

"What a nice guy," said Bo. "Helping a friend out like that."

"You just can't leave things around here on the street, officer," said the burglar. "Could get stoled."

The burglar laughed. Tommy smiled. Bo was stony.

"What's this friend's name?" asked Bo.

"He not exactly a friend."

"What is he exactly?"

"Just some guy from the neighborhood. I don't know his damn name."

"He's your friend, he's not your friend, he's from the neighborhood, and you don't even know his name?" said Bo, advancing a bit, applying just a touch of pressure, a hint of menace, leaning just enough in the direction of making this an official interrogation to make the burglar see that there could be trouble ahead.

"From the neighborhood. Just some dude. He aksed me to watch his set. Oh, man, look at this shit. Some motherfucker akses me to watch his fucking TV set and now all this shit comin' down on me."

"You gotta admit, it looks a little funny," said Bo. "Someone else could misunderstand. I mean, it looks bad, you sitting out here on top of what may prove to be stolen property. Unless you have a bill of sale in your pocket. Do you have an authorized bill of sale in your pocket?"

"Take it easy, Bo," said Tommy, playing the good cop.

"I do not believe this shit," protested the burglar, getting down from his TV perch. "Try to do someone a favor and look at this shit. You can take the fucking TV set, man. I don't give a shit."

"Why don't we wait for your friend?" said Bo, hard.

"Take it easy," said Tommy, the peacemaker, the reasonable party searching for a way out. Then, as if he were trying to change the subject, Tommy got down to business:

"We're not after a TV set. We're looking for a burglary team."

The burglar nodded. He looked relieved.

"There's two guys," said Tommy. "Black guys. One tall. One short. The short one limps. They're from around here."

Ask the same set of questions a couple of hundred times and you get to hear the denial before it is even uttered. You get to expect the disappointment and start to walk away before it even happens. But this time, the earth stopped rotating.

"Yeah, I know them," said the young burglar.

Bo and Tommy stood there and the young burglar nodded, puffed on his cigarette, and grew easier, feeling the safety of a greater interest. They really were after a team.

"They from across the street," said the burglar.

He used the burning end of his cigarette to point to the tenement at 62 East 125th Street, on the north side of the street.

"Tall one's named Harold. He lives in the front. First floor."

"The short one?" asked Tommy.

The burglar shrugged.

"He don't exactly live there. But he's always there. I mean, they always together."

"Listen, my friend, get lost," said Bo, looking across the street at the building. "Vanish for a while. And do not open your mouth. We know you. You get my drift?"

* *

It was one of those early tenements, built in the twenties, when the decorative arts were still lavish, even in modest construction. Before the Wall Street crash. Once, it was a proud middle-class building. There were flourishes in the cement. But the pride had eroded with the cornices. Now rows of locks ran down the reinforced steel doors like military buttons. Behind the iron bars, the windows were cracked and filthy. The hallway smelled of garbage and urine—the stench of social exhaustion.

Bo and Tommy walked in cautiously, not really believing that they were close to a solution. It would have been too big a stroke of luck.

From the front apartment, they heard a burst of laughter. Then the high-pitched squeal of delighted teenagers running wild. The door was open and Bo could see the kids smoking pot, drinking wine. They were having a party. He and Tommy pushed the door further and stepped in and the music stopped, the laughter stopped, the noise stopped. Someone yelled, "Cops!"

"Hey, no big deal," said Bo, with that young, forgiving baby face. "Smoke what the fuck you want to smoke. We're not here to bother anyone."

They were high school kids. Fifteen, sixteen, seventeen years old. They were getting a running start on a long weekend. There were about ten of them scattered around the living room.

"Come here," called Bo. "I want everyone to come here."

They were suspicious, but they came when Bo called. They were a little afraid, but not much. It was only a possible pot bust, and nothing worse was going on.

42

Then Bo said: "We're looking for a team of guys, one tall, one short. Burglars. We know they live around here. The short guy limps."

They looked at each other. They looked baffled.

"Hey, mister, we don't know anybody like that," said one, maybe the kid who lived in the apartment.

"Guy's name is Harold," said Bo.

"Harold?" asked a girl. "No Harold here."

"Yeah, he's supposed to live here. Tall guy. Hangs with a short guy."

"Don't know no Harold," said the girl.

"There's a tall guy lives upstairs with his stepfather," said another girl. "But his name isn't Harold."

It always falls apart, just when you can taste it, they both thought.

"What's the tall guy's name?" asked Bo.

"They call him Chicago," said the second girl.

A flare of hope again. Chicago isn't a person's name.

"Does he hang with a short guy?"

"Yeah," said the second girl. "He has a short friend."

"The short guy has a limp, am I right?" asked Bo.

"Nah," said the second girl. "No limp."

"A limp," said Bo, who began to try to imitate the limp, stumbling across the floor. "You know, a limp."

"No limp," said the second girl. "He bops."

Bo and Tommy looked at each other and blinked. A sudden understanding burst upon them both.

"You know the way they do," said the girl. "He bops."

Bo imitated an exaggerated knee dip, the kind of ghetto salute of someone who marches to his own cooled-out drum.

"That's it. That's Max."

"Max?"

"That's the short one."

There was an extension cord leading from the apartment to the hallway socket. Someone was stealing electricity. They pounded on the door and it was answered by a giant. The guy stood over seven feet tall with shoulders so large he had to stand sideways to get through the door frame. He looked down at Bo and Tommy without a trace of fear, despite the fact that his apartment was cluttered with a lot of stolen goods with price tags and inventory-control tags still attached. It was the apartment of a fence.

"What the fuck do you want?" asked the giant.

Bo and Tommy looked up.

"We are not looking for any problems," said Tommy for openers. "We are not out to bust you for any shit—"

"That's good," said the giant. "For you."

"We're just looking for Max and his friend, Chicago. You know—Harold."

"What do you want with them?"

Bo thought quickly. He remembered that there had been a burglary on the police blotter. Some fool had robbed Nicky Barnes, known popularly as the "drug kingpin" of Harlem. To steal from Nicky Barnes was to invite death. "They fucked with the wrong guy," said Bo. "They robbed Nicky Barnes. Hit his disco across the street."

"Stole all his stereo equipment," chimed in Tommy.

"Not smart," said the giant.

"So Nicky's people are looking for them," said Bo. "They're out to kill their ass. You seen them?"

44

The giant stood for a moment, then spoke. "Not this week." He pointed down the hall. "Stepfather lives over there."

The old man with a glass eye was making coffee. He set out the cup on an unsteady table. The tabletop was alive with roaches. Bo and Tommy sat on old tubular stainless-steel chairs with cracked vinyl backs. In another room, a four-year-old girl in a soiled nightdress played on a bed.

Bo showed him a police artist's sketch of the man. He didn't tell him why he had a sketch of his stepson. Just said he was looking for Harold.

"Why you after him?"

"Look, we don't know if he had anything to do with this thing, and we can't tell you exactly what it is, but he's better off talking to us."

"Well, I haven't seen Harold all week."

The little girl in the other room was watching daytime television, and the sound of the soaps drifted into the kitchen where Bo and Tommy sat on the edge of the vinyl seats.

The old man with the glass eye moved his head to favor the good eye, to see better, as Bo handed him his business card. "If you hear from him, here is my card," said Bo.

The old man took the card and put it on the table, among all the roaches.

Chapter 6

There's a lot of frustration here. We are this close to nailing these scumbags. This close. And then it's nothing. It's gone. We'll never hear from the stepfather. I know it. We'll never see Harold Wells, who is probably in Australia with his friend, Max, who is demonstrating his "bop" down under. All we have is a pound of shit. So there's a lot of frustration.

We're driving away and we can't go to the Colonial because I just don't feel like running into that Italian heat—Fat Tony and Fish riding my ass about when the fuck I'm gonna bring these guys in. I just don't wanna hear it. So we're driving near the Joint Disease Hospital on 123rd Street and there's a crap game out on the street. Right out on the street. And they know we're cops, right? These guys know me. And they know Tommy. So I am driving along and I stop the car and Tommy asks me what I am doing. There are these fifteen bad fucks shooting craps in my face and I am steaming. I am sitting in the car and I gotta say something:

"You guys know who I am! I'm not gonna lock anybody up for playing craps, but you should stop the game until we pass. You should show me a little respect."

One big guy is sitting there, guy with a shaved head. Mean-looking guy. "Fuck him, man," he says. "Fuck him, shoot the dice!"

I say, "Hey, we are the police. You know who I am." And the guy with the shaved head says, "Fuck you."

I put the car in park and get out, and Tommy is saying, "Oh, Bo, don't get involved. Let it go."

I stick my head back in the car window and say to Tommy, "You know I always get involved." Tommy is meanwhile unlimbering his second gun, 'cause he senses trouble. He carries a 9-millimeter semiautomatic, along with his regulation .38-caliber piece. I walk over and I kick the dice. I say, "Why are you doing this to me? Why are you treating me like a piece of shit? You know who I am. You know who the fuck I am. You know what the trouble is? We have no respect among each other here."

So the big bald guy says, "Why don't you go fuck yourself, you little punk."

Tommy is out of the car. All the other guys are laughing. And the bald guy is still sitting down saying, "Fuck you. Go fuck yourself." He's a bad dude. I know him. He had just gotten out of Sing Sing where he was Joey Gallo's bodyguard. All mobbed up and mean as shit.

So, now this guy is sitting down. I have no idea of his size, although I know that if he's taller than me sitting down, he is one big fuck. I say, "Go fuck me? No, fuck *you," and he takes a swing and boom! I smacked him in the face. He started getting up and my eyes start rolling around watching him get up. I am saying to myself, "Holy shit, what the fuck am I getting into?" He's got hands that look like bricks. All of a sudden one of these bricks hits me in the face. My nose starts to bleed and we are punching away at each other. All the other guys are yelling and I hear Tommy in the background. He's got his 9-millimeter out and he's Duke Wayne again. "Okay, everybody stay out of it. This is a fair fight."*

Fair fight my ass, call for help.

This doesn't take long. We both get in a couple of good shots. I know he can take one and he knows I can take one. He's got another kind of smile after this. Like he's saying to himself, "This is one cool motherfucker"—I took his best shot and I didn't lock him up after he whacked me. So I walk away and I say, "Next time show a little respect."

I get into the car and drive away. I'm bleeding all over myself and I say, "Tommy, don't you ever do that again." He goes, "But I knew you had it all under control, partner."

There were thunderclouds over East Harlem that Friday afternoon. Soon the sky would open, but it didn't stop Bo and Tommy. Nothing could. They were tired and frustrated and, most of all, they were desperate. They stopped in shops and hounded store owners. They interviewed random pedestrians. They cashed in every chip that they had outstanding. And nothing connected. Nothing seemed to lead to something. And throughout, they were unable to shake the thought that they had neglected some plainly marked trail, that something tangible had slipped through their fingers.

When the rain finally came, it was actually soothing. Refreshing. Cleansing. Bo, in his leather jacket and dungarees and construction boots, was beginning to grow ripe. He told Tommy that he thought oil was actually coming out of his hair.

They couldn't stop because then they would have to confront their peers. They would have to listen to the rough ridicule that Bo had invited with his boasts. They were like a Flying Dutchman, cursed to wander the streets until they solved the case.

It was dark, ten o'clock at night, when they got the signal, ten-one, over the radio—call the station-house.

It was Lieutenant James Geary, a friend, who was lonely. "What are you two up to?" he asked over the land line.

"I don't wanna talk over the phone," said Bo. "I'll tell you when we come in."

"Pick me up," said Geary. "We'll go over to the Colonial and have some dinner."

On their way over to pick up the lieutenant, Bo was gloomy.

"We missed them," he told Tommy.

"Maybe it wasn't even them."

"It was them," said Bo. "I know it. I can feel it. You know me when I get that feeling. We had 'em and we let 'em get away."

"What else could we do?"

"I don't know. Something. That fuck was lying."

"The stepfather?"

"The stepfather. The fence. Every swinging dick."

"We still got a shot."

49

"No. We missed 'em."

"C'mon, partner, where's that old Bo Dietl spunk?"

At the Colonial Bar on 116th Street and First Avenue, Bo consoled himself with cold fish salad and linguini with white clam sauce. He washed it down with wine. And he killed all care with silver bullets—vodka on the rocks. Tommy didn't even bother to touch his food. Just the Johnny Walker Red and soda.

"Is that all you're gonna do, liquidate your body?" Bo asked.

Tommy didn't speak. Bo picked up a forkful of linguini and force-fed his partner. "If you don't eat, I don't speak to you."

And Tommy chewed without tasting, swallowed without desire.

"You two," said Lieutenant Geary, shaking his head. "You're like an old marriage."

"We had it, Lieu," said Bo, between bites and swallows. "We had it right here." He held out his beefy hand.

The lieutenant shrugged. "You didn't have much, Bo."

"I had the feeling."

The waiter brought another round of drinks. Bo waited until he was gone, then leaned over so no one would overhear. "You know about my feelings, Lieu."

"I know," said Geary, concentrating on the food.

"My partner had it right," said loyal Tommy.

The waiter returned and whispered into Bo's ear. "It's a ten-one," said the waiter, an old cop fan who knew the code calls.

Sergeant Stevens, their anti-crime boss, was on the land line at the stationhouse.

"I been trying everywhere for you guys. Listen, you got a call, Bo."

"Yeah?"

"Some guy. Says he wants to talk to you."

"Yeah?"

"Says he's the stepfather. On One Hundred and Twenty-fifth Street. Says you'll know what that means."

"The stepfather? Really?" Bo couldn't keep the excitement out of his voice. Sergeant Stevens heard it half a mile away at the precinct.

"Listen, Bo, I want to be in on this," said the sergeant. "I don't want this a Wild West operation. If it's good, I think I should be there. For your sake."

"That's fine, Sarge."

"Why don't you pick me up?"

He was jumping in, but Bo didn't mind. They might need an extra cop.

Back at the table, Bo said, "Sorry, Lieu, we have to go."

"You gotta go, you gotta go," replied Geary, who knew that something big was on. "But I wanna finish my dinner. I'll catch a ride from somebody else."

Tommy understood what was happening without being told. It was written on Bo's face. As they left the restaurant, the lieutenant called after them: "Let me know what happens."

Bo turned.

"We gonna get these sons-of-bitches!"

Bo and Tommy picked up Sergeant Stevens and were on their way back to 125th Street when a ten-thirteen came over the radio. One of the anti-crime units was in trouble. Everything stops when a cop is in trouble, even this. The anti-crime team was chasing a couple of armed robbers. One of the gunmen was caught. The other had vanished inside an abandoned building. The building was a block and a half away from 62 East 125th Street, where the stepfather was waiting to hear from Bo. It was still raining hard. Bo looked at his watch. It was eleven o'clock.

We're standing there with our guns out and all I am thinking about is the other thing. Why am I wasting my time with this bullshit? "Let's go in," I say. "No," says someone, one of the bosses. "We'll wait for Emergency Services."

I said, "Fuck Emergency Services. C'mon, Tommy." Tommy gets out his 9-millimeter and we go, one, two, three, right through the fucking door.

The guy is standing there, scared shitless, watching these two wild men break in the door. He throws his gun out the back window. We get him, cuff him, turn him over to somebody. "Don't you want the collar?"

I yell, "You take it," and we're off. Tommy and me are operating like an orchestra now. We don't even have to speak. He knows what I'm thinking and I know what he's thinking. We got a mission. This is the peak, this is the best, the finest moment of police work. It's like pulling a perfect double play, or maybe it's Fred Astaire and Ginger Rogers. I can turn my back, I can go through doors, because I know, I know, my partner is in back of me, he's watching out for me. We can do anything together. So my confidence now is zooming.

The old man was waiting.

"Come into the kitchen," he said.

He looked as if he were in pain. And he was. He looked down at his hands in which he held Bo's business card, with the name and the official shield of the New York City Police Department embossed on the front. It seemed like a long time until he spoke:

"If he had anything to do with it, I want to know about it."

"What are you talking about?" asked Bo.

The old man looked up into Bo's eyes.

"Well, after you were here today, he came back with his girlfriend, Sugar. I told him you were by here. Bo and Cowboy, I said."

Bo and Tommy were on the edge of their chairs. Sergeant Stevens stayed in the shadows.

"Where is he now?" asked Bo softly.

The old man ignored Bo's question. He'd answer in his own fashion. "First thing he says, 'Could I borrow some money?' Says he's going home to Chicago. Had to get a Trailways bus and go home to Chicago. And I lent him the money."

The old man looked up, trying to impress these strangers with the extent of his moral dilemma. He spoke simply.

"It's been on my mind. I sat here thinking. Then I called you at this number." He held up the card, worn thin by the pressure of the old man's grip.

"If he had anything to do with what they done to that nun, I want to know."

I looked at Tommy and Tommy looked at me. Stevens was just watching. Something incredible had just happened and we all knew it. Our hearts were in our throats. First, because of this gutty old man. Took a lot to do what he did. And you could see what it cost him. But most of all, now I know that this is our guy. I said, "Oh, my God," and I gave the old man a big kiss.

Chapter 7

They returned to the Twenty-fifth Precinct station-house in a state close to frenzy. Sergeant Stevens ushered Bo and Tommy up the stairs into the dead midnight of the squad room.

"Don't utter a word," he said. "Not to anyone."

He needn't have worried. The only people in the squad room were the overnight skeleton force of detectives finger-painting paperwork.

Stevens pulled Bo and Tommy into a small office and locked the door behind them.

"Look, you're not going to like this, but we need the grown-ups," he said.

Bo knew what he meant. He wanted administrative muscle, someone who could muster support. He also wanted to protect his ass, which, at this stage of the game, looked like it might be significantly extended. Bo looked at his watch. It was 11:45. "Sarge," he said evenly, because he had his own priorities fixed, "I'm not arguing, but we got a hot suspect on a bus to Chicago."

"I know that," replied Stevens crisply. "Don't you think I know that?"

"Every second counts," urged Bo. "Every second of that clock, he's getting away."

"A few minutes won't make a difference."

"It might. It just might."

"Now we need the big guys, Bo. Now!"

Bo looked over at Tommy, who nodded. Sometimes, even the brave have to bend to procedure.

"Call Lieutenant Crean," said Stevens.

Lieutenant Crean was the head of the precinct's detective unit. Crean had the authority and know-how to rally the troops, to organize a team, to coordinate the various agencies, which circumstances seemed to require.

"We got an out-of-town thing here," explained Sergeant Stevens. "We're not just pushing in doors. This is interstate."

"Okay," said Bo. "Okay. But let's work sensibly. You call Crean. I'll get Sex Crimes. This is still a Sex Crimes case, right?"

"It's still their case."

Bo dialed the Sex Crimes Unit, but the phone kept ringing. There was no answer.

"Can you believe this?" he said, shaking his head. "These guys are off for the weekend. We got a massive case here and nobody is working. Nobody is manning the phones."

It was getting very close to midnight and Harold Wells was getting closer to Chicago. Once Wells got off the bus, they might lose him forever, they might never be able to find him again. Everyone in the room understood that. Especially Bo.

He put his ham fist down on the desk. "Sarge, we are not going to let Harold get away. I don't give a shit about stepping on toes or whose nose gets pushed out of joint. You call who the fuck you want to call. I'm going after Harold Wells."

Bo made a few calls and roused the head of Trailways Bus Company. In minutes, he was able to establish that a bus bound for Chicago had left Manhattan at 5:30 in the afternoon—which fit snugly into the time frame established by the stepfather. If Wells had told his stepfather the truth, he and Sugar were aboard that bus. It would arrive in Chicago at 6:30 in the morning.

When he heard the coincidental details of the timing, all of Bo's skin tingled with certainty. He knew that Harold Wells was aboard the bus. And he knew that Wells was the nun rapist. He had no proof beyond long inferences and the thrill of intuition. Nothing that would hold up as "probable cause" in a court of law. But he would bet his life on it. He was already risking his career.

"It's for you," said Sergeant Stevens, pointing to the phone. "On three."

Bo pushed the blinking button.

"This is Lieutenant Crean."

"Yes, sir."

"You have something hot?"

"A conflagration, Lieutenant. We got the rapists. I know it."

"Call Sex Crimes."

"Yeah, well, the trouble is nobody answers."

"What?"

"There's nobody there, Lieutenant. Their phones are dead. They musta taken the night off."

Sergeant Stevens, listening, poked the number three

button on his telephone console and joined the conversation. "That's right, Lieutenant. Nobody's there. We called already."

"All right," said the disgusted lieutenant. "Call Inspector Sibone. I'll be in as soon as possible."

"Yes, sir."

There was a frantic scramble to find Inspector Charlie Sibone, the head of Manhattan North Detectives. Finally, they reached him at his home.

"I'm sorry to bother you, Inspector—"

"Who is this?"

"Officer Dietl, sir, up at the Two Five."

"Bo! How the hell are you? You know, you are one terrific cop. I have been meaning to tell you. That subway thing and catching those stickup guys was terrific work—"

"Thank you, sir, but we have a situation here and we need some backup."

"Oh?" He had his defenses up—as if Bo had shifted the conversation and was now trying for a loan.

"It's the nun case, Inspector."

"The rape?"

"Yes, sir."

"That belongs to Sex Crimes."

"Yes, sir. We tried. Nobody's there. They took the night off."

"What have you got?"

"Frankly, sir, as far as hard evidence, I've got a pound of shit."

Sergeant Stevens covered his eyes. Tommy smiled. Bo went on:

"But I've got a very powerful feeling. I know we've got it cracked. We got one guy on the run. You know there were two guys, right? One tall. One short. A burglary team. Well, me and Cowboy found two guys.

The short one with a limp. When they heard we were on to them, they turned rabbit. We know that one of them—the tall one—is on his way to Chicago. He's on a bus that gets there at six-thirty in the morning."

He laid it out, leaving off the part about Nicky Barnes because if he included that, Sibone might dismiss it, might conclude that Harold Wells was running from Nicky Barnes. But this was Friday, and Nicky's business took place on Monday and Harold only started to run after he heard that Bo and Cowboy were after him—not Nicky Barnes.

It didn't take Inspector Sibone long to grasp the situation.

"Okay. Listen, Bo: I am authorizing you and Detective Colleran to get on a plane and fly to Chicago," he said in his best official voice. Then in his best friendly voice he added, "Follow him, Bo. Don't let him get away. We'll get Sex Crimes to catch up with you. And Bo?"

"Yes, sir?"

"It sounds good."

The high command of the police department was now on notice that a major breakthrough had probably been achieved in a case of overwhelming importance. However, no one notified Jimmy Sullivan, the chief of detectives. It was an oversight that would rankle him and cause a spiteful aftermath. This was not on anyone's mind at the time. Under the deadline pressure, Bo Dietl did not worry about departmental protocol. He was trying to catch a moving bus.

This was the autumn when the air-traffic controllers were on strike. Airline schedules were in chaos. Service to Chicago was spotty.

"We don't have a plane until morning," said an

airline's representative. "Earliest flight out is seven o'clock. That doesn't get you there until after nine."

"This does not help," said Bo, hanging up.

Meanwhile, the detectives from the special task force assigned to crack the case began to filter into the precinct. Word was spreading throughout the city by that mysterious police rumor network that works quicker than satellite communication, that something volcanic was going on up at the Two Five. There were first-grade detectives wandering all over the squad room. But none seemed to know what step to take next. Each in his turn was briefed. Each went through a stage of disappointment that it had not been he to crack the case. But then they rallied, each and every one, and tried to figure out where they could catch a little remaining glory. They made phone calls and talked tough, but no one had the first idea of what to do.

Except Bo and Tommy.

It was one of those monkey scenes again. Everybody walking around with a banana up his ass. So I leave everybody. I go into the lieutenant's office and I pick up the telephone and I ask the operator for the area code for Chicago. Then I call information and I ask for the number for the police department. I dial and I get, "Chicago Police Department Emergency." I say, "I want the Detective Bureau." So they say, "Well, we are the Violent Crimes Section." I said, "That sounds good."

You know fate's a funny thing. Or maybe it's just cops knowing about other cops. I make a call and I get a Sergeant Kelly. He gets on the telephone and he says, "Sergeant Kelly here, Violent Crimes Section." Just that sound—you know, an old cop sound—and I knew I found a friend. I felt a little safer.

"How are you doing, Sergeant Kelly? This is Bo Dietl from the New York City Police Department."

"Hey, how are you doing, Bo? What's this about?"

"You know, we had a thing that went down here about two weeks ago—a nun was raped."

"Oh, yeah, we know about that. It was all over our newspapers. This was in the convent."

It had not hit Bo until that moment that this was not a local outrage. The story had national and international resonance.

"We know all about it," said Sergeant Kelly, a veteran of twenty-eight years on the force, Bo had learned.

"Let me tell you what I got," said Bo in that familiar litany of his. "I got nothing. Nothing legally. But I got a feeling. And you been a cop for twenty-eight years and you know what that is. Legally, I cannot hold the guy, but I definitely have a feeling. This is one of the guys."

"What do you need?"

"I need to make sure he doesn't get away. I have to question him. I can make a seven o'clock flight, but his bus is gonna be arriving at six-thirty."

"You want us to pick him up?"

"No. Just follow him. We'll rendezvous with you when we get there."

"You got it," said Kelly.

At 6:00 in the morning, Inspector Sibone walked into the squad room. Bo gave him a quick update.

"We got one guy good. A whole shitload of priors."

"What about the second guy?"

"Just a first name. Max."

Sibone looked at his watch.

"You guys gotta make that first flight out of here," he said. "Where's Colleran?"

Tommy had gone out to get breakfast for the entire command. He had gone to McDonald's and wasn't back yet. Bo was itchy, but he wasn't worried. It was only 6:30 and LaGuardia Airport was five minutes over the bridge. It struck him that Harold Wells's bus was pulling into the Chicago terminal at that precise moment.

At 6:30, Tommy had not yet returned with the breakfasts and Bo was getting ready to leave without him. He was not going to travel alone. He had to take along a Sex Crimes Unit detective anyway since only the Sex Crimes Unit knew what questions to ask Harold Wells. No one yet trusted Bo enough to give him the details of the crime. All he knew were little snippets he picked up from eavesdropping.

Suddenly the phone rang.

"Hey, Bo Dietl, phone call for you from Chicago."

Bo picked up the phone. "Officer Dietl here."

"Hey, Bo, it's Sergeant Kelly. Listen, the bus got in early."

Oh, shit, thought Bo, they lost him.

"Yeah, but no sweat, we got your boy."

"What are you talking about?"

"We got your boy. In custody."

"You weren't supposed to grab him."

"No, Bo, it's okay. He confessed. The whole thing. He talked about the nun on the third floor. Gave us all the details. Everything you'd want. The way they did it to her. The pew. The whole thing."

It took a minute to sink in. And then Bo began to scream.

"They got him! They got him! They got him!"

He was dancing around the squad room and lifting fat detectives out of their chairs and kissing them smack on the lips.

Inspector Sibone asked: "What happened?"

"He confessed," cried Bo. "Harold Wells confessed. To the whole fucking thing. He gave details, everything."

"This is going to be a special promotion with the police commissioner personally attending," said the inspector.

Bo remembered the phone. He ran back and picked it up.

"Kelly? Are you still there, you big Mick?"

"Yeah, Bo, I'm here. Is it all right? You don't mind that he confessed, do you?"

"Kelly, I love you."

Chapter 8

Tommy was coming back, carrying twenty of those plastic trays from McDonald's. He bought breakfast for everybody. He's walking up the stairs, heading for the squad room, and he didn't know yet. Now, I had to tell him. I had to let him know, because he's part of this. So I run down to meet him and, bang! I hit the trays underneath and they go flying. I spilled McDonald's breakfast all over the fucking staircase. It was a shower of eggs and sausage. And, of course, I'm yelling. "We got him! We got him!" Inspector Sibone is hugging and kissing me and hugging and kissing Tommy.

"Oh, Tommy," I say, "we're saved. We're fucking saved!"

Forget the fucking parking tickets. Forget the petty complaints.

Little did I know. The Chicago police did not exactly play by the rules. They did some freelance questioning on their own and they may have been a little rough. Frankly, I think they stuck a gun up his ass.

But, hey! I didn't give a shit. Not at the time. Listen, they didn't play by the rules when they raped the nun, did they? The fact is, we got them. We got the right guys. That's what's important to me then.

We go back into the squad room and everybody is beaming and applauding. I am sitting there like a fucking rooster that just fucked twenty-seven chickens.

But there's something I gotta do. I grabbed the keys to the unmarked radio car and I sneaked downstairs. I stole the car and I just go. I do not tell anyone where I am going. I put the light on top of the car and I put the siren on. It is seven o'clock in the morning on Saturday and I am running down 116th Street with the light and the siren going and I am screaming out the window. "We got him! We got the guy who raped the nun!"

The people are all going to early mass. The church bell is going, Bong! Bong! Bong! and I'm screaming my heart out: "We got him! We got him! We got the guy who raped the nun!" I stop the car and get out and the old ladies in black who are up in years in the Eighties and Nineties are hugging and kissing me and we're dancing in the streets. I stop at Marone's Bakery between Second and First avenues—the best Italian bread in New York—and they're trying to push free bread in my hands. I run over to Vinnie Rao's house and I ring the bell. He moves a little slow, and I go, "Vinnie, we got 'em!" And there are tears in his eyes. I give him a big kiss.

I wake up the whole neighborhood. The whole neighborhood. I go into the Colonial—I don't give a shit. Everybody gets hugged and kissed.

From seven to eight that Saturday morning, I was dancing over the whole neighborhood. I owned it. I was running around like a nut, but that hour was sheer ecstasy. It felt like the whole world was in love with me. For one whole hour.

And then it was eight o'clock and Bo was back in the squad room with one suspect in Chicago and another one on the loose. Sergeant Kelly was on the phone again.

"Hey, Sarge, when I get you in New York, I am going to buy you the biggest steak you ever saw."

"I'm from Chicago, Bo. We fucking invented steak."

"Okay, pal, lobster, caviar, whatever you want."

Two men who had never seen each other sounded like the oldest friends in the world. And, at that moment, they were.

"Listen, Bo, we wanna check and see if he gave us the right name on the second guy."

"All we have so far is Max," said Bo.

"Max Linderman. That's what he told us."

Tommy, who was listening on the extension, broke in. "Hold on. I know that guy. I locked him up a few years ago. He's a black guy with a Jewish name. Sticks in my mind."

There was a long rap sheet on Max Linderman. He was a junkie and a burglar. For another hour, they all sat around the squad room, staring at records, tinkering with reports, accepting the applause and phone calls from the downtown brass. It was a sweet, hazy, luxurious bath of appreciation, but they had to pull themselves together. They had unfinished business.

"We gotta bring Max Linderman in," said Bo, pushing the paperwork aside. "He's gonna hear that we got Harold and then he's gonna go deep. Let's get organized. Let's coordinate this fucking thing."

The suspect had an address; they could check the

address. The suspect had a face; they could print up his picture and pass it out to the cops on patrol. The suspect was a known drug addict. They could check the known drug locations.

"He's out there," said Bo, in his overheated dramatic fashion. "Let's get him."

There were, inevitably, a lot of abandoned buildings in Harlem. The impoverished tenants would fall behind in the rent and the landlord would give up trying to collect or make repairs. Finally, the landlord would walk away, abandoning his property. And the building would gradually die. First the electricity would be cut off. Then the scavengers would pluck out the pipes, forcing the water to be turned off. The tenants had no choice and would move away. Soon the city, in an attempt to discourage homesteaders, would seal the doors and cover up the windows with sheet metal, like putting pennies in a dead man's eyes. And like worms, the junkies would crawl into the corpse of the dead building. These dead, infested buildings became the "known drug locations."

They hit them in tactical style. One in the back to cut off retreat, one in the front. Mostly the junkies were harmless slaves to their addiction. Too feeble to resist. But every now and then they ran into "crack" killers. And so care was always exercised.

"We're looking for Max," said Bo.

He had them up against the wall, their shadows flickering by the candlelight. There were six of them. Tommy had them covered with his 9-millimeter. The filthy needles were spread out on a soiled blanket.

"Max!" shouted Bo. "We're looking for Max."

The junkies looked dazed. They always looked dazed, especially when they were wrenched out of their drug stupor. They were only attentive and alert when it came to the actual moves for getting a fix.

"His name is Max," repeated Bo. "He runs with Harold, a guy named Harold. They call Harold Chicago!"

Bo walked over to the blanket and stepped on the loaded needles. He could see the pain, the loss, in their faces as they watched the dope destroyed. Now they understood that there would be a price to pay for shielding Max. Under that kind of pressure, sooner or later, someone would give him up. But they didn't know him.

They hit three such locations, then came back to the stationhouse to see if anyone had had better luck.

Just as they came in, there was a phone call from Max Linderman's mother. She told Sergeant Stevens that she heard the police were looking for her son. She said that he was willing to surrender and that they could pick him up at her house.

Bo couldn't go when they went to pick him up. He had to wait for another call from Chicago. Sergeant Kelly had some details he wanted to pass along. He would only pass them along to Bo Dietl.

Tommy and Stevens went. I am still getting my head screwed back on straight. But I stay behind and they go and they have no problem. He surrenders like a lamb. So he walks into the stationhouse and I looked at him when he walks in. And he knows me. And he gives me a fucking smirk.

We go into the back interrogation room and I am sitting there and the Sex Crimes Unit guy arrives. We're ready to talk to him. The first thing out of the guy's mouth is, "I do not like you." To me, right. He says, "Go fuck yourself."

Well, actually, he didn't say that right away. I said a few things first. Like, uh, "Oh, you're no more big man, are you? You got cuffs on now, you little fucking weasel. We got you good, huh?" I did say a few things, which is normal considering what we had been through and the nature of the crime.

So he says, "Go fuck yourself," to me. I take the cuffs off, that is, I uncuff one hand. The cuffs are still on one wrist. He is not handcuffed like he later said. But he definitely did not have handcuffs on when he went after me. I admit that I slapped him, but he went after me first. I slapped him across the face. Knocked him across the room. Actually, I think what happened is that I automatically went into the good-guy/bad-guy routine without even knowing it. I was playing the bad guy.

Tommy pulled me off. "Let me kill the little motherfucker," I yelled.

I was tired. I was up for three days. And the guy was trying to hit me. And I slapped him. I really believe he was trying to hit me. That was the end of that.

So now we start the interrogation, good-guy/bad-guy. It went on for about two hours. I would stay out of there because he did not like me. I felt like we were getting nowhere with me in there.

I tried to talk to the little creep. I said, "Listen, Max, just pretend, okay? Imagine what it would have been like to rape the nun." He'd be quiet, but I'd start to get crazy. Because when I suggested that, I started imagining him raping the nun. I got all kinds of pictures in my mind and then I wanted to eat his fucking lungs. It was not a good tactic.

So I left Tommy and the Sex Crimes guy to do the interrogation. I was behind the two-way mirror. Every time he got cocky, I'd open the door and pretend I was going to come back into the room.

Then they pulled me out. The hotshots from the task force were there now, watching with me through the two-way window. Then, all of a sudden, it strikes me—he's going into this trance. He's putting himself into this state, like an angel dust trance. He's not even there. He's feeding them all this shit about how he's innocent, he's the wrong guy. In other words, he hasn't broken yet.

Then the detectives in the room with me are picking it up. I hear them saying we got the wrong fucking guy. The cops in Chicago fucked it up. Waste of fucking time.

Now I am starting to second-guess myself. Is it possible I made a mistake? We don't have anything solid yet. What do I have, really? Nothing. I am beginning to doubt my own strong feeling. I am beginning to really sweat.

But then, thank God, I hear it in the next room. Max's voice, so soft, so matter-of-fact. The first-graders aren't even listening anymore when Max says, "Well, we were smoking dust. And I remember going to the convent. And all I remember was grabbing the nun . . ."

So I turn to all these first-grade detectives, all these hotshots who are making fun of me, and I say, "Hey, you scumbags, hey, you dumb cocksuckers, get your ears over here. We got the wrong guys, huh, shitheads? Listen to this, you assholes!"

The ADA, Linda Fairstein, head of the Sex Crimes Division, takes me aside. They were matching up things from Chicago. "You got the right guys," she said.

Oh, God, the second stage of that rocket kicked in. I was in outer space.

Chapter 9

Bo Dietl didn't know it, but his triumphant moment was about to end. The department snipers were zeroing in on the very thing that he thought protected him—his success.

By midafternoon, the press began to assemble in force outside of the stationhouse. There were reporters and photographers and camera crews milling behind wooden barricades in that exquisitely patient modern ritual, the media stakeout.

Bo saw it as a festive table laid out to satisfy his healthy appetite for acclaim. "Look at this," he told Tommy. "Have you ever seen so many photographers?"

"I wonder what brings them into this neck of the woods?" said Tommy.

Bo and Tommy were monitoring the arrivals from a second-floor window, looking for the possible arrival of the mayor, when one of the task force detectives came over and said, with a kind of casual force:

"Look, there's no reason for you guys to hang around anymore."

Bo was stunned. That they should be dismissed—as they certainly were—at the prize moment was a slap in the face. It was a violation of one of the most time-honored police customs, which is to give the grunts in the field who break an important case the proper credit. Like a mention in dispatches.

The traditional tableau was repeated and frozen in countless newspaper photographs: the suspect in the middle, head bowed, playing his role of mortification. On the flanks, holding the handcuffed prisoner by the arms so that society could see plainly that he was safely in custody, were the unsmiling hero cops, with their police shields flapping proudly from their breast pockets. No chief. No politicians. Just cops.

It was a cliché, but it served a purpose. The picture apparently satisfied some deep hunger of the public's to see the culprit in the hands of his captors. Editors looked for it. No important arrest story was complete without it.

But Bo and Tommy were being pushed out of the picture.

"We'll handle it from here," said the first-grade detective.

"Fuck 'em," said Bo as he pulled Tommy away from the squad room. "They want to steal our case, but we know what we did. Fuck 'em."

They went to the corner bar and sat in the same spot that they sat in four days ago when their future looked bleak. Tommy was hugging Bo and crying.

"I can't believe it," he said again and again. "I cannot fucking believe it."

"They'll never take your shield now," said Bo.

"They can't take away what we did, partner," blubbered Tommy. "They can't take that from us."

Bo was buying drinks for the house.

"This is a fucking dream," he said. "Slap me and get me out of this dream."

"I cannot believe this," said Tommy.

"Which part?" asked Bo.

The *New York Daily News* is an old tabloid newspaper whose reporters are said to be half cop and half journalist, and no one is certain, in a pinch, which side tips the balance. The undeviating code of that newspaper is to celebrate the police department whenever possible. Thus, the *Daily News* reporter, who knew the standard procedure when an important arrest was made, was curious to know where the heroes were. He was met by blank stares.

And when he asked, "Who broke the case?" there was an embarrassed, foot-shuffling, throat-clearing silence as the chiefs and deputy chiefs stumbled over an explanation.

"We're not releasing that yet," was the official line.

Daily News reporters are trained like bomb-sniffing dogs to look for police heroes, not evasive chiefs. And so he poked around and persisted and kept asking, "Who broke the fucking case?"

Finally, someone who hadn't gotten the word blurted that "Bo and the Cowboy" broke the case.

"Where are they?"

"Probably at the corner bar celebrating."

Which is where the reporter for the *Daily News,* along with a reporter for the *New York Post,* found Bo and Tommy.

The drinks were flowing and the reporters' notepads grew fat with colorful versions of the exploit.

I had just seen the Blues Brothers movie—you know, where they said that they were on a mission from God—and this reporter from the Daily News *is interviewing me and I'd had a few, you know? So I said, "You know, we were on a mission from God." And the next day's story began with the line, "Two cops were on a mission from God."*

Everybody in the bar was clapping me and Tommy on the back and telling us what a great job I did. Even this one chief. Not a bad guy. He's in there with us, getting half bagged, hugging me and saying I'm gonna get a special promotion for this and they're never gonna take away Tommy's gold shield. Not after this, not after what you two did.

I say to Tommy, "We better go home and get squeaked up a little. We look like bums. But let's be quick. I don't wanna miss anything." See, I still think there's a chance we're gonna get what's coming to us. I still believe in justice and fair play—this is why I'm a cop in the first place. I still can't believe what happened.

So I'm driving home in my car and "Don't Fall In Love with a Dreamer," which was a big Kenny Rogers hit that season, comes on the radio, but this is no dream. I fly through the house and get back in an hour. From Queens. When I hit the Two Five, there's this sergeant from Sex Crimes and he hands me the keys to the car and says, "Go warm it up." Meanwhile, they bring Linderman out the back, to another car. When they take a picture of the prisoner being led out, I'm warming up the wrong car.

I know I'm being fucked, but what I can't see is the behind-the-scenes shit. I hear later that the chief of detectives, Jimmy Sullivan, is out for blood. He's ready to fucking kill. All the trees in the forest are gonna fall, that's how mad he is.

And why? What's the big excuse for this violent temper tantrum? Because nobody called him. His little feelings were hurt. Nobody notified him about the arrests and he wound up looking like an asshole. So when the police commissioner, McGuire, calls him up on the morning of the big arrest and congratulates him, and says nice work, Sullivan says, "What are you talking about?" And the commissioner says, "You know, the nun case. Great job."

And the word that filters down later—what I hear— is that Sullivan had no fucking idea of what he is talking about. Not a clue. Well, it was an oversight. There was a lot going on. Somebody thought somebody else was gonna call and it turned out that, in the end, nobody called. You could see where he might be miffed—after all, he is the chief of detectives and he is supposed to know if there's a break in a monster case—but to ruin so many careers, to break so many men over a petty fucking detail, well, it just seems like an overreaction.

So Sibone gets knocked back into uniform. The head of Sex Crimes gets thrown into the Two Eight. And eventually, they take Tommy's gold shield away. As for my promotion to detective, well . . . I heard a lot of things over the next few months.

Tommy Colleran was back in uniform and Bo Dietl was working decoy, still wearing a white shield. He and Tommy received awards from the governor and from civic leaders. When they were named Cop of the Month by the *Daily News* they received the award from Mayor Koch on the steps of City Hall. No police brass were present, though usually the police commissioner attends. There were luncheons and dinners and plaques. But there was no gold shield.

Bo kept hearing that he was going to be promoted, but it was always another month away. In January, there were some questions to be cleared about Bo's off-duty work, acting as a bodyguard for the royal family from Saudi Arabia. When there was no impropriety found there, they had questions about brutality complaints. When no foundation was discovered for these complaints, there were unexplained, vindictive delays.

In February, there were hints that the promotion was being questioned because he was a friend of Tommy's and Tommy was a scofflaw.

"What's that got to do with me?" he asked a superior on the promotion board.

"You were his partner," replied the superior.

"What is this, guilt by association?"

"You're not entitled to a gold shield, Bo. No one is entitled to a gold shield."

"I am."

The funny part is that Bo would probably have been made a detective by Christmas if he hadn't broken the nun rape case. That previous summer, the summer of 1981, he had made three important bribery arrests. A man who murdered another guy and then tossed the body in the East River tried to give Bo several thousand dollars, as well as a pile of jewelry, to let him go.

Then there were two dope dealers, in two separate instances, who tried to buy their freedom. Bo just tacked on additional charges.

There is nothing that pleases the police department more than proof that their members—subject to endless temptation—are incorruptible. There is even a special board called the Bribery Review Board empowered to reward cops who resist such temptations. Bo Dietl certainly qualified for this route to his detective badge.

When Bo appeared before the board in September, it looked as if he were one step away from a gold shield. "It was something very deep with me," he had told the panel. "I could never take money. It has something to do with not disgracing the department. I hate cops who gave other cops a bad name."

His record was good, and when he answered the grand jury charges of brutality in October, it looked as if the path were clear.

But that promotion got shredded in the bureaucratic blizzard that followed the nun case. It was a strange Catch-22: Bo was supposed to be promoted for his great detective skills, not his virtue. In the end, he demonstrated both and was stuck in place.

At the start of May 1982, almost seven months after the nun case, Bo got a call from a friend at the Bribery Review Board—a panel made up of the superchiefs: chief of patrol, chief of detectives, chief of operations, etc. This was the highest-ranking panel within the department. They met rarely to consider special cases, to promote deserving cops outside of the regular career path. Bo's friend had been telling him that the promotion was imminent. The phone call in May was to report that the board had met and considered Bo's case.

"I got some bad news for you," he told Bo.

"What happened? I thought they were meeting today?"

"They met," said the friend, a little embarrassed. "They said they wanted to give you a letter of commendation from the police commissioner."

"That's it?"

"That's it, Bo. I'm sorry."

"They want to give me a letter? After twelve years?"

"Take it easy, Bo—"

"You told me what you had to tell me. Thanks."

Bo hung up. "Those motherfuckers," he said.

See, the reason I was so mad was that I paid for that gold shield. It was mine. I spent twelve years, putting my ass on the line, trying to become a detective, working decoy.

No one knows what that means. Not unless they've been out there, sitting in the fucking bull's-eye. You sit out there in some doorway that stinks of piss and vomit and you wait. You wait until the cramps in your legs feel like a knife and you pray they'll turn numb. But you can't move because you'll blow the decoy—the bad guys are watching to see if you move. They can be very patient, these bad guys.

So you have to sit there and live through that knife and you try to control the muscle spasms. And do you know what you're waiting for? You are waiting for someone to break open your head. That's what they do to test you, the people who want to lift your wallet. They hit you over the head to stun you, to see if you'll react, to see if you're a cop.

But even after they whack you, you can't move. Not yet. You have to act like you're really passed out drunk—maybe moan a little. But you can't leap up and grab 'em. All you'd have was a simple assault. You want that fuck for theft as well as assault. You want that felony because now you have a grudge. So you wait for the hand to go into your pocket after the wallet. And when it comes, it is the best fucking feeling. God, it feels

78

good. All the pain, all the cramps are worth it just for that feeling. That's when I knew I had them. When you actually felt that, only then would you go into action. Then you'd make the collar. That's what it is to work decoy. The guys on the job knew that.

In twelve years, I had well over a thousand felony arrests. The average cop makes 120 in a whole career. And my collars were good; 95 percent stuck. That was my conviction rate.

So, by my own personal accounting, I figured that I earned the gold shield. I got receipts—the broken bones in my nose; the scars from the knifings; the concussions. I got joints that creak like an old man with arthritis. I paid in blood and bone for that shield.

But it wasn't only that. See, I was out there in plainclothes acting like a detective. People thought I was a detective. But I was not a detective. And that was bad. I kept saying, "Next month, next month." Four times I planned a party. Four times I had to cancel. My friends asked me why I wasn't a detective, and when I would tell them why, they would look at me like, "Yeah, sure." I did not have the gold badge and that was the end of it.

Captain Louis Fortunato was down at the end of the hall. He heard Bo yelling. He heard the curses. He knew what it was all about.

"Give me a 28," demanded Bo.

A 28 was a form requesting time off.

He took it down another hall and threw it in front of Sergeant Stevens. "Sign it," he said. Stevens also knew what was going on. He signed the form.

"Now I'm on my own time," announced Bo.

Muttering, Bo drove down the East River Drive,

heading for One Police Plaza, headquarters. "They did it to Tommy and now they're doing it to me," he muttered darkly.

Bo saw that he was moving ninety miles an hour. He didn't care. He was in a controlled rage.

He left the car defiantly eating up two spots in the reserved lot outside of headquarters. And he barged into the anteroom of Chief of Police Operations Murphy.

"I want to speak to Chief Murphy," he told the receptionist.

"Do you have an appointment?"

"No, I do not have an appointment."

"The chief is busy."

"Just see if he'll see me."

"Who should I say?"

"Bo Dietl."

The receptionist went inside, then came out. "He does not want to talk to you."

"Thank you very much," said Bo, turning and taking the elevator up to the thirteenth floor, where he asked to see the police commissioner.

The lieutenant on duty at the reception desk said, "Who are you?"

"I am Bo Dietl."

"Oh."

Bo didn't know that Captain Fortunato had called ahead, warning the brass that Dietl was on his way down and in a dangerous mood.

"Officer Dietl, you have to make an appointment."

"Oh, I do? Well, here is my badge." And he laid his silver shield on the desk, turned, and planted himself on a couch. "Now I'm a civilian."

"Officer Dietl," began the lieutenant.

"Listen, don't tell me anything anymore, because I'm not a cop anymore."

A captain named Scott came out from an inner office and he picked up Bo's shield. He stood there with the shield in his hand.

"What seems to be the problem?" he said.

"Look, Captain, I don't want to hear any more bullshit. I'm tired. I'm tired of being humiliated. And I have been humiliated. My partner has been humiliated. We break a case that we should be rewarded for, we should get a pat on the back, and we get nothing. I can see why people walk off this fucking job. No more bullshit. I am not leaving."

The captain looked down at the shield in his hand. "Calm down, son," he said. "We know what's been going on. We know what's happening. Give us one day."

He moved to hand the shield to Bo and Bo took it.

Chapter 10

The next morning at eight, Bo Dietl's supervisor, Captain Louis Fortunato, sat squirming in that cushioned sanctuary, the office of the police commissioner.

Fortunato had been summoned and instructed to bring all of Bo's records down to headquarters and now he suffered miserably while Robert McGuire read through the documents.

It took some time since the folders were bulky. The commissioner studied the letters of commendation, the awards, the long string of evaluations, as well as the accusations of rough handling contained in the personnel folder. But McGuire was the son of a cop and he knew that it wasn't always possible to find the truth about a policeman in the strangled, bureaucratic jargon of a personnel folder. There were some cops who piled up impressive records and were, at bottom, hollow self-promoters. Often enough, a good cop could wind up buried under an avalanche of spite.

And so McGuire turned to Captain Louis Fortunato, Dietl's commanding officer, and asked a simple, pertinent question:

"What kind of cop is Bo Dietl?"

Fortunato had been through the ups and downs with Dietl, watched him plan then cancel the parties to celebrate his promised promotion. He shared Dietl's frustration.

"He's the greatest cop I ever had working for me," he said without hesitation.

There was a pause. It was stuffy in the large office with the pictures of past commissioners staring down like anger from the walls.

"Would you say that he's rash?" asked McGuire, alluding to the outburst of temper that propelled Bo to leap over the chain of command and bring his case directly to the commissioner.

Fortunato took his time answering. "Most cops are obedient and live by a strict code of conduct," he said. "They know what to do because the book tells them what to do. But there are a few who live by the skin of their teeth. They see a thing and they react. It's not calculated. Maybe it's instinct. Maybe it's emotion. But it's usually for the sake of justice. They have a very clear idea of what they consider right and what they consider wrong. You could call it rash or you could call it leadership. I don't know. I do know that Bo Dietl is such a cop."

The commissioner nodded vaguely.

Captain Fortunato added something: "And he's been treated like a yo-yo."

"The greatest cop you ever had in your command?" asked McGuire.

"I mean that, Commissioner."

"Without reservation?"

"None."

"Must be quite a cop."

"Yes, sir."

They both smiled.

Bo was pacing in the squad room when Captain Fortunato returned and motioned him to follow him inside his private office. Fortunato then closed the door behind him.

"You have to be down there tomorrow morning at nine-thirty," he said.

Bo was suspicious. "What for?"

"It's something that they've never done before, not in the whole history of the police department. They're going to have a special session of all the superchiefs. They're going to hear your case."

"Do I take a lawyer or what?"

Fortunato shook his head. "Just you. You'll be alone with all the superchiefs."

There was a memorial service that Friday morning for all the policemen who died in the line of duty. The chiefs came straight from the ceremony. They sat across a vast table in the conference room in their dress uniforms—the stars of their rank blazing in Bo's face. The three-star chiefs—Sullivan, McCabe, who now is chief of patrol, Chief Courtney, Chief Guido, and Chief Vivoda. And Murphy, chief of operations, with his four impressive stars.

Bo was wearing a civilian suit and his palms were wet. He felt as if he were sitting across from seven slabs of stone. He sat at attention.

Chief Murphy spoke first. His voice was crisp: "Why did you decide to become a police officer?"

"I wanted to help people."

It is almost impossible to explain it to a row of cement blocks. These guys want to hear that God whispered in your ear. It doesn't sound good to describe it the way it really happened, which was an accident. One day, you're hanging out with your friends in Ozone Park in blue-collar Queens. Half these guys got fathers and uncles and cousins on the job. From the minute they're born, they're gonna be cops. Cops run in cop families. They say it's because of the pension and the benefits, but it's not. It's something else, something different. You look at a guy and say, "Cop." Period.

So, anyway, it's a summer afternoon, somewhere between high school and a job or the army, and we're hanging around after coming from the beach and somebody says, "Hey, you comin' on Saturday?"

"What are you talking about?"

"Saturday. We're all going down to take the test for the cops."

"No shit?"

"Arencha comin'?"

"Me? Nah."

"C'mon. We're all going."

And before you know it, it becomes a challenge. Everybody is going. Everybody's gonna take the test for the cops. So Bo Dietl has to go and take the test to keep them honest, to show that he can do it.

It sounds like something casual, a whim, when you put it like that. But I don't believe that it was a whim. I took the test for the cops because I was one of those people you could look at and say, "Cop." Period.

Bo didn't like the answer he gave to Chief Murphy. But he was not clear about the reason he became a cop. It was complicated and lost in his own childhood.

Still, he tried to make them understand: "The reason I wanted to be a cop was I hate bullies," he said.

"What's that?" asked one of the chiefs.

"I hate bullies; I can't stand it when people are afraid," explained Bo. "When they're afraid of a gang or somebody, I hate it. It's got to be ended. I can't stand it when there's an outstanding bad feeling. I hate it when people are mad at me. All my life, I tried to make it come out right."

My father had arms like lampposts. It was all that lifting of slabs of meat, all that cutting up of salads. He was a cook. Tremendous arms. Strong. That's where I get my strength.

When he came home from work, he'd ask my mother what I did wrong, and even before she could say anything, he'd be taking off his belt. It had a big metal buckle. FD. Frank Dietl.

I never understood why he was so mad at me. I know the man had a lot of problems. He was a gambler. Once he even lost the house. My mother never let him forget it. Every time they had a fight, she'd say, "Remember the house."

I remember once he left his job. When I was a little kid, she didn't believe him when he said he had a job at the airport. She made him take me when he went to pick up his paycheck. I remember the car ride. I remember that he left me outside and went into an office and pretended to get paid. But she was right. He got the money from Household Finance. He was always in hock to the finance company. She'd find the slips in his pockets when she cleaned out his pants. And she would start screaming at him and he would stand there in that stubborn German way. She was Sicilian and he was German. What a pair!

He never talked much. I never really had a conversation with him when I was growing up.

I remember when he hit me. It was because of my looks. I looked too much like my mother. My brother had that Aryan blond look, but I was dark and Mediterranean and it really made him mad. I guess he was trying to whack the Sicilian out of me.

But he couldn't change my looks. He couldn't even make me cry. He was frustrated. My old man hit me a lot. Every single day of my life. Until my seventeenth birthday. That's when it stopped. He came home from work mad, as usual. He had some complaint—I don't even remember—and he went to swing at me. I caught his arm in midair. I was pretty strong by then. I caught his arm and I held it. He could feel the strength in my arm. "That's it, Pop," I said. "No more." He never raised his hand to me again.

When I got older, I'd try to tell him that I understood. I'd tell him that I loved him. And he would pull away. After his stroke, when he couldn't help himself, I'd pick him up in my arms like a baby, like I was the father, and I'd kiss him and hug him. He couldn't stop me. He couldn't pull away anymore. Like I said, I can't stand it when there's a grudge, when someone has a mad on, when it doesn't come out right.

One of the superchiefs had a confidential report in front of him. It contained a familiar vial of gossip, a poison that seemed to haunt Bo's career.

"You know, people say that you got some help in working on the nun case," said Chief Sullivan. "The word is that members of organized crime tipped you off and you sat on information."

"If you'll forgive me, Chief Sullivan, but that's a bunch of crap. I got no help from members of organized crime. I didn't even get any help from the precinct detectives."

"Officer Dietl, there are reports that you have acquaintances who are members of organized-crime families," said another chief.

Bo knew the accusation and he knew the basis for it. He answered with a sigh:

"I grew up in Ozone Park, which, as you know, is an Italian and German neighborhood. I went to school with some kids. I later heard that their fathers were members of organized-crime families. But I didn't know them as criminals. I knew them as fathers. Good fathers."

Chapter 11

The house was a nice house. Not fancy, but it felt comfortable. Bo was always struck by the perfume of garlic and veal when he came through the door of this ordinary house on an ordinary street in Ozone Park.

Sometimes there would be a strange car parked in the neighborhood, filled with guarded men in boxy suits with plain, out-of-state looks. The men in the cars would note license plates and sneak pictures and remain locked inside their cars. These were the FBI agents and cops who staked out the ordinary homes of senior executives in what was known as organized crime.

Bo was not curious about the activities of Phil, the man of the house, nor, for that matter, any of the other men who belonged to the hunting and fishing clubs with blacked-out windows sprinkled throughout the area. He heard the stories of how they ran rackets and controlled hijacking. But he was born into a neighborhood conspiracy of disbelief. As far as he was concerned, they were the community leaders. They always dressed "nice" and they always treated him with respect. He could not imagine a bloodbath being ordered by such soft-spoken men.

Phil, who ran several labor unions and was alleged to be connected to the Colombo and Genovese crime families, genuinely enjoyed the company of Bo Dietl —a respectful and clever youth. Bo came over in his T-shirt, and, after his long workouts in the school gymnasium, seemed to embody robust health. It was a stark contrast to Phil's own younger son, who was hooked on a heroin habit.

I started coming to the house for dinner as a friend of the son. The kid had a problem with drugs. I was a couple of years younger than the son. But he liked me; all the kids liked me. They trusted me. I used to hold their arms when they shot up dope. I guess that was a kind of honor, to hold their arms.

The older brother liked me because I was ballsy and because I didn't shoot up dope.

The older brother's name was Tony and we became friends. I was tough and they liked guys who were tough.

I had a reputation. I earned it early. When I was eight, there was another tough kid in school. He was eleven. So we had a fight over who was the toughest kid in the school. This was an important topic in the schools of Ozone Park.

This was the first fight I ever lost. The guy had me on the ground and he was punching me, banging my head into the ground, and he keeps saying, "Give up? Give up?" I didn't say a word.

He opened up my head pretty good—I am bleeding

everywhere. But I don't give up. The kid's only eleven and maybe he's tough, but he starts to get scared. I mean, he begins to think maybe he damaged my brain, maybe I can't say uncle. Finally, he gets up and he backs away and he is definitely more scared than I am.

I realized that I had this extra power. This ability to take a punch. I wasn't afraid.

Three years later, I took on the same kid again. It was no contest. This time I had him on the ground and he said uncle very fast. By then I had a reputation and the kids I looked up to, like Phil's son, liked to have me around.

One day, when I was about sixteen, maybe seventeen, there was a thing with a motorcycle gang. I was with my best friend, Ronnie Streppone, and I'd borrowed a prize MG from another friend. Ronnie and I were parked outside a hamburger joint and this guy from the motorcycle gang leans on the car. So I told him to get his fucking ass off the car. We had words, he smacks me with brass knuckles in the face. I start to bleed pretty bad, and I smack him, and I see the guy's seconds running away. Then I hear he wants to meet me and fight.

We're gonna meet at this old wooden bridge over in Howard Beach. Tony is gonna drive me to the fight. So we go by Tony's house and he jumps out of the car and comes back and he's got a paper bag and inside are two .38s. They're loading the guns in the car and I'm saying, "Hey, I want to fight the guy. We don't need the fucking guns. Just let me fight the guy."

"You don't understand," says Tony. "They're not going to fight. They're going to kill you."

Tony tells me to stay in the car when we get there. But I say no. I want to fight. He says there is no fight. Tony and this other guy—they called him Lord Fox; he's dead now—will handle it. I have to promise to stay in the car. All of a sudden, when we get there, they get out and start walking; they're getting close to the bridge, and this motorcycle comes out of nowhere and a guy with a machete tries to slice Lord Fox in half. Fox knocks the guy off the motorcycle, picks him up, and tosses him off the bridge. Tony and Lord Fox, two of them, took on these eight mean fucks. Kicked the shit out of them. They were the toughest guys I have ever seen. Not afraid of anything.

They would have killed them, but police cars come screaming in from all directions. Our guys have their guns out and the cops grab them and take them inside this tollhouse on the bridge. In a minute, they come out. The cops released them. They knew who they were.

In the summer of 1968, when he was seventeen years old and had graduated from Richmond Hill High School, Bo was a little lost. He'd been turned down for a gymnastics scholarship from Springfield College, in Massachusettes, because his grades were too low. He didn't have a job or a destination. His usual impatience was running at top speed. He had come to see Phil for guidance, for support, for the calming effect Phil exerted on him. Bo did not speak as much as listen respectfully.

"So, tell me, Bo, what will you do now?"

"I don't know, sir. I guess I need a job."

"I thought you were going to college."

"I was hoping for an athletic scholarship, but it didn't come through."

"A shame. Nice kid like you."

"I suppose I'll find a job. I like to work."

"You like the money."

"I do. But I also like to work."

"What kind of a job?"

"I don't know, sir."

Phil nodded. In his world, all communication seemed to be conducted on some unspoken levels of reconciling meaning and need. Understanding was a measure of wisdom. Phil was accustomed to the sort of oblique appeal for help that Bo seemed to be making.

Of course Bo knew that Phil controlled aspects of the construction trade through his union connections. "Fine," he said. "Tomorrow you go to Thirty-fourth Street and Lexington Avenue."

"What's there?"

"A hole in the ground. You see Sammy-the-Weasel. Be there at seven-thirty. You will start work at eight."

"I don't know how to thank you," said Bo.

"Just don't be late."

They were erecting a thirty-eight-story luxury apartment building at Thirty-fourth Street and Lexington Avenue. There was a small wooden shanty on the site and when Bo went in, he found Sammy-the-Weasel drinking coffee. Sammy turned his back on Bo, a comment on the long hair and the headband and the cutoff jeans. When Bo mentioned that he was sent by Phil, Sammy stubbed out his cigarette, put down his coffee, and made Bo a member of Local 6A of the Laborers Union.

By eight o'clock, Bo was making $7.50 an hour plus benefits.

Bo made certain that he earned his money. He

arrived on time and left late and pulled more than his share of the load. In fact, he enjoyed all the physical tests that construction work demanded. He unloaded the hundred-pound sacks of cement four at a time. "Put another one on," he'd tell the skeptics on the truck, and they would take bets about just how many sacks it would take to break the back of the hippie with the washboard belly.

And he was amazing. After staying up all night partying, he'd show up before dawn and start doing push-ups on the high steel. He'd tighten up his stomach breaking three-by-fours. For fun, the ironworkers bet him that he couldn't move the huge cement bucket. Ordinarily, men couldn't budge the thing. It took a crane. But Bo moved it and bought beer for everyone with his winnings.

Sammy-the-Weasel watched over him, saw to it that no one took advantage of Bo. Bo got his share of overtime, as well as his share of time off. It wasn't only the fact that Bo was a personal friend of Phil from Ozone Park—although that didn't hurt. The truth was that Bo was likable. He was friendly and cheerful and didn't hide down in the well.

It wasn't long before Bo was working as an ironworker and began earning eleven dollars an hour.

One day, when they were working on the high platform, Sammy-the-Weasel had a heart attack. Bo helped bring him down. He kept thinking: He's not old; a man in his fifties. Bo looked around and saw men in their thirties who looked defeated. Their skin was all wrinkled and rubbery. Hands would tremble from too much liquor or too much strain. It took a toll.

You don't read about all the casualties in construction—they're buried in tiny boxes on the back pages of newspapers. A man falls to his death here. Another is crushed under falling debris.

During his time working in construction, Bo watched four men die in front of his eyes. The men on the construction sites had a peculiar indifference to the losses. Almost as if they had calculated this as part of the payback of the big paychecks.

One of the first things I did was to go out and buy a new car. I'd been driving a beat-up old Volkswagen. I called it the one-eyed monster. But now I was making four hundred dollars a week, kicking in eighty to the house, and I felt entitled to a new car. The car I always wanted was a Corvette. A bomb. But, you know, I just couldn't go that far. It was too much.

Finally, I decided to get a Plymouth Sports Satellite. I couldn't get it on my own. I didn't have the credit. So my father went down with me. And he cosigned the note. This was the first time my father had talked to me like I was a man. He said, if you want the Corvette, buy it! I was so happy my father was now treating me with respect.

That summer passed in a blur of hard work. Bo would head home after a long day on the site, one hand on the steering wheel of his new Plymouth and two barbecued chickens in his lap. The bones would go flying out of the window as he headed along the Long Island Expressway.

The police department kept calling, asking if he was interested in becoming a cop. Bo didn't return the calls. The test slipped from his mind.

Meanwhile, Bo rediscovered his fear of heights. He

had been a kid when he first recognized it. A kind of queasiness. But he thought he had conquered it. His brother Alan, who was always close to Bo, had dared him to walk a dangerous ledge on a building in his neighborhood. It was a two-inch ledge and he had circled the building. He even made himself look down, in spite of the dizziness.

But when he was nineteen, he worked the high steel on the World Trade Center and the old pale qualms returned. He waited until the job closed down for the night, then went back up, six hundred feet in the air, and forced himself to walk the narrow steel beams. If he did not entirely conquer his fear, he did hold his ground.

It was winter. And it was cold up there on the steel. The wind coming off the river feels like cold death. There's no way to keep warm. I kept thinking, This is no way to spend your life. This is too quick.

One night, I get home and my mother tells me that the police called again. They said that this was the last time that they were gonna call. If I didn't take the job, I would be dropped from the list. She was all for me becoming a cop. She thought that being a cop was a great job. It had prestige. It was a step up. After freezing my tail off up there on the Trade Center, I saw her point.

They sat in the social club on 101st Avenue as they had sat many times before. Phil asked about the job and Bo thanked him again and said it was fine. They spoke of this and that.

"I gotta tell you something," said Bo.

Phil nodded. He knew something was coming. He could sense it all evening.

"I have decided to become a cop."

Phil looked, for the first time since Bo knew him, genuinely surprised.

"You are going to become a fucking cop?" he cried.

"Yes, sir."

Phil laughed and slapped his thigh.

Chapter 12

Only the parched sound of paper being turned broke the stuffy hush of the conference room as the chiefs leafed with vague, unfocused anger through the personnel folder of Bo Dietl. Each had a copy before him and they turned the pages as if they were looking for an incriminating clue.

"Your name is Richard Dietl?" asked Chief Murphy.

"Yes, sir."

"Not Bo."

"Not officially."

"But everyone calls you Bo."

"Yes, sir."

"Why do they call you Bo?"

"When I was a kid, I had a problem with names."

They looked at him—those unforgiving department chiefs with faces imbedded with suspicions, frowns frozen into accusations—as if they had caught him red-handed in some criminal deceit. Using an alias. As if the false name itself were proof of wrongdoing and bad character. An aka (also-known-as). In their world, criminals hid behind false names. It was therefore a natural assumption, an old habit to these flinty men, that Dietl had something to hide.

"I don't understand," said the chief.

"Well, sir, in school, I was popular. Kids would come up to me all the time and say, 'How you doin'?' I couldn't remember all their names. I didn't know what to say. So, I just said the first thing that came into my head. I said, 'How you doing, Bo?' Pretty soon, everybody started calling me Bo. And that became my name."

He shrugged and smiled at the three- and four-star chiefs who sat there, in their Mount Rushmore scowls, treating the story as one more phony alibi to be broken.

Among the guys, when I was a kid, I always tried to be a hero. Always someone that they admired. I was strong. I was a good athlete. I was also the class clown, saying something smart to the teacher. I always raised my hand in class. That's why the kids would know my name. And I wanted the attention. I liked it when I could feel the eyes on me when I walked down the street: I was noticed.

My father wasn't in good health in those years. Strong, but not athletic. Then, in 1958, something happened. His gallbladder exploded and he went down to a hundred pounds. He almost died. Me and Alan had to go away for the summer. A Catholic camp. Run by nuns. I was eight, Alan was ten. It was the first time we'd been away from home. I mean, without our parents.

I remember going to the bus station. My father was still in the hospital and my mother put us on the bus and I was excited. Alan was crying, but I was excited. I kept saying, "Everything's going to be all right. Don't worry. I'll take care of everything. Nothing is going to hurt you."

And I loved it. Alan cried all night, every night. Some kids picked on him. These were older kids, but I went over and said, "Don't pick on my brother." They told me to get lost and I hauled off and punched one. Then they all jumped me and I started pounding away.

They stopped picking on Alan after that. And he started to get confident. No one would pick on him because then they would have to fight me. And I liked to fight. I fought every day of my life. I was always in a fight. But it was always a good cause. I was always on the right side.

The camp was great. It was hard living. There was no hot water. We had to do everything with cold water. And the food was gruel. Nothing that you'd ever want to eat. This was the first time that I ever had contact with black people. I mean, close contact. Most of the kids there were black. And they were good kids. One or two, I couldn't get along with. But that's true of everyone.

I would take off in the woods. Being on my own was great. I was never afraid that I couldn't find my way back. I always knew that I'd be okay. I don't know why, but I had this tremendous confidence. I could do anything.

Not everyone had the same confidence in me. One

day I was in the camp hospital, sick, while everyone else went on a hike. My parents happened to call and whoever was in the office couldn't find me. They forgot to put my name on the list. So, naturally, my parents thought I was lost.

I was sitting at the window of the hospital that night and I looked out and I saw my father coming across the lawn. With a cane. Bag. Drainage. Everything. He walked out of the hospital and came up and brought me home. But I really liked that camp.

We lived in an old house that took a lot of work. My father was always fixing or painting it. We had an old porch out front. Old and wood, like you don't see anymore. One day, before I was eight, we were getting ready to go away on a trip. My father would drive to the Howe Caverns, Niagara Falls—whatever. I liked the trips. I liked going places.

So, on this one day when I am six or seven, we are all getting set for the trip and I hear something on our porch. A noise. Something. You can't explain these things. Whatever I hear at that age tells me that it's wrong. It was some guy stealing the beach chairs from the front porch.

Well, my father starts after him, but this is a young guy and he's fast and eats up my father. But I chase him. I am a kid and I am chasing this big guy.

After a couple of blocks, this thief drops the chairs and really takes off and I lose him. I have no idea what I would have done if I caught him. But that did not enter my head. All I remember is that I had to chase him. I couldn't let him get away with stealing our beach chairs.

And I remember that I wasn't afraid.

"You became a trainee in 1970."

"Yes, sir. January 2, 1970."

"You remember dates?"

"That one sticks."

I reported to the auditorium of the Police Academy on Twentieth Street off Third Avenue two days after the New Year. New Year. New decade. New job. I got there early because I was excited. I could tell right away: I liked it.

There was an atmosphere of importance. And strength. A lot of strength. Like some monster fucking engine that could do anything. All these big, tough guys walking around with guns, right out in the open, wearing them on their belts. Guys in suits wearing guns! Like businessmen carrying pens. All this power. God, it was impressive. Yes, I knew instantly that I liked it.

First thing, you start going through the physicals and the examinations. Then they start giving you the lectures. Most of these trainees were the kids of cops. I mean, they knew what to expect. Their fathers and uncles told them what it would be like. I was like a fish out of water compared to them. I didn't know any of the jargon or stuff like that. But I made myself learn. I learned very quickly.

The bad part was that you were going to be getting four thousand dollars a year. I was used to twenty thousand. I don't know how I'm gonna live without the difference. You get used to money, you know. You have to be twenty-one to be appointed a regular policeman. That means I'm gonna be a trainee for two years. But the excitement was there. Right away. And I knew that I would work it out.

"Your first assignment as a trainee was the Hack Bureau."

"Yes, sir."

They give you a brief orientation—mostly threats that if you screw up you'll be thrown out. Then they give you a token and send you down to become a flunky in some command that needs gofers. I was assigned to the Hack Bureau, which is located on Hudson Street. A gray dumpy old warehouse converted to office space.

Now, there was a cold-water treatment, as far as an introduction to police work. I get there and it is like a bomb hit these people. Everybody looks a little dazed. A lot of these cops are broken-down valises. Psychos. Cops with big drinking problems.

But I don't care. I got a taste of the job. I show up in my grays—they called us mice—with my trainee manual and I am bug eyed. I loved it. I loved the badge. I loved the feel of it. Buy a quart of gin and some rummy cop'd let you have his badge for the afternoon. That was an incredible feeling, walking around with a real cop's badge or a detective's badge. You could walk into subways for free. You could walk into movies without paying. Having a real badge was like being Superman. You could walk through walls.

The first job they gave me was filing. Some of the trainees liked that. They could daydream or get lost for three hours. But I liked the window. This is where the cabdrivers come to apply for a license or to get a replacement for a lost or chewed-up license. It's where the action is, which is where I like to be. They line up and it can get very emotional. These guys are trying to make a living and if they think that they're being fucked over, they can get a little excited. Which is why I liked the window. I got to the point where I was doing things that a lieutenant is supposed to do. Like replacing lost cards. I had the power to replace a lost card. I couldn't see some poor bastard losing a couple of days' pay while he waited for a lieutenant to get to his case. So I just did it. Now, if I was corrupt, there was a chance for real money in that job. They'd put bills between the folds of the application. But I'd just give it back.

"Oh, listen," some guy would say, "I just got my license suspended for thirty days. Here's twenty dollars."

"You got the wrong window," I'd say.

"How much will it cost?"

Not that they were wrong. There were a lot of guys stealing. It was crazy. Here we were watching the Knapp commission hearings on television—they were being broadcast every day while I'm there. There's David Durk right up there on the screen saying that the department is corrupt, there's Serpico giving lectures about honesty and morality, and all these lost cops at the Hack Bureau are saying, "Lying scumbag!" At the same fucking time that they're saying this, they are taking money under the table to process applications! Insane.

But not me. I was incorruptible. Besides, I was having too much fun running the window. You'd see guys coming down, balls of fire, and you'd have to tell them, "Look, get on the line. Calm down. We go in order here."

And they'd give you some shit and you'd say, "Listen, get on the line and keep your mouth shut or we're not going to wait on you."

Once in a while you'd get some guy who'd go berserk. Couldn't take all the hassle. There was this one guy I remember who wouldn't stop cursing. I tell him, "Hey, there are women back here!" Now, this is bullshit. The women who worked in that place had heard it all. I mean, there is nothing on this earth that you could say that they haven't heard before. In much more colorful terms. But I say, "Hey, there are women back here," and that puts the guy on the defensive. Now he's wrong. Unless he's a complete degenerate wacko, which this one guy was. He keeps going and keeps going and finally I say, "Okay, that's it, I am not going to wait on you." He tells me to come outside and say that.

I go outside and he comes after me and all the other guys—the real cops—come storming out. It's like the first time they had to act like cops in years and they're ready to shoot this poor fuck. They grab the guy and they got him cuffed and they're gonna lock him up forever.

"Let's go in a back room," I say.

We get in a back room and they leave us alone. Maybe they think I'm gonna beat the shit out of him, but I wasn't. "Listen," I say, "you shouldn't treat me like that in front of people. I represent authority. You make me look like an asshole."

The guy becomes very contrite. By now he's also a little worried because he has seen guns in his face. He's got handcuffs on. He comes outside and apologizes to the women. He apologizes to the men and to the people on line and to me. I didn't have to have him locked up. I didn't have to hit him. All I had to do was defeat him psychologically.

I was learning to be a cop.

I loved the job and I worked hard, but I needed money. So, on the side, I kept working construction. I wasn't supposed to, but I wangled time off. I pulled weekend duty and piled up overtime. I worked six, seven straight shifts. I had two and three months off at a time.

Now at this time you had the hard-hat demonstrations in support of the Vietnam War. It was the Honor America Day thing. We marched down to City Hall. At Pace College you had these long-haired students who started throwing rocks from the roof. They were anti everything that was Honor America. So we ran in after them and they tried to close the glass doors and we busted the glass and chased them and there were some fistfights. But they didn't throw any more rocks.

I felt pretty good after that. Along the line of march, there was a bar with exotic dancers. I went into the bar and pulled out one of the dancers and she came along with us.

The next day, on the front page of the Daily News, there is a picture of me, and on my shoulders is one of these exotic dancers wearing my hard hat. Everybody at the Hack Bureau saw the picture and they're saying, "Hey, isn't that you, Bo?"

I look at it. "Nah! I admit, it looks a little like me. But that's not me."

There was a guy working in the Hack Bureau who I never got along with. He had a thing against me. He had to check me out. There's always one guy who wants to see if you're really tough.

I notice this. I can see it in this guy's eyes. He's a broken-down detective and he never does shit. He comes to work every day and the first thing he does is to pour liquor into his coffee cup. And every day, he tells me to do this and do that. Do his filing. Type out his reports. This guy is a detective and I'm a trainee, but finally, I've had it. "Listen," I say, "I don't have to take your shit and I'm not gonna do your job."

"Yes, you are," he says. "You're a fucking trainee and you do what I tell you to do."

"Go fuck yourself," I say.

So he grabs me by the front of my shirt and I take his hand by the wrist and I start to squeeze. I can see his face and he is in pain.

"Don't fucking grab me," I say very low, because I don't want the others in the room to hear me, I don't want to humiliate the guy. "Don't fucking touch me. And don't ask me to do your fucking job."

I could see by the look in his face, he won't bother me because he knows I won't take his shit. If he goes to the lieutenant, then he's gotta answer for not doing his job. And the lieutenant knows and the sergeant knows about his drinking and they also know that I'm doing the work of two or three guys.

There's always one guy who's gotta test you, who's gotta see what you're made of. When I went to Communications, there was another. But I put a stop to that right away.

"You were there for seven months and then you were reassigned to Nine One One."

"That's right, sir."

"These evaluations rate you very high."

"I enjoyed the work, sir."

There was a freeze on hiring after the Knapp hearings. I was sent to Communications. I was getting a little tired of the Hack Bureau anyway. It was clerk work. But Nine One One, that was real police work. Now I am starting to get into the real stuff. You get on the phone and you take calls from these people who are in bad trouble. Somebody's dying, somebody's breaking into their house. I was cool and good and they put me right on the radio. I was dispatching cars, taking charge, feeling great. I loved coming onto that radio.

"Hello, fellas, this is Bo."

And all over the city these guys'd come back on the air. "Hey, Bo! How ya doin'?"

"We got a busy night tonight. Forty calls outstanding, but we're gonna clear it up, bing! bing! bing! and then have some fun."

Technically, this is all a violation. There are proper radio procedures and I am not following them. But all the guys got to know me and respect me, because I know what I'm doing. What they do not know is that this is a nineteen-year-old kid controlling sergeants and lieutenants all over the city. They think I'm an old pro.

The great thing about that job is that you learn everything about police work. You learn the whole city. You have your finger right on the pulse.

Shots fired? Send a car and backup. Get a ten-thirteen? Send in backups from adjoining precincts. Make sure help gets going. That goes right to the top of the list. Take care of the cops. Guys out on a chase, give them a well-done afterward. Remember that these are human beings out there, putting their ass on the line.

After a while, after they got to know me, some of the guys want to meet me. They wanted to see this guy Bo Dietl who was running the whole police department, calling in helicopters, bringing in the Harbor Unit.

We arranged to meet in a bar in Queens and they were really surprised. They saw this young kid and they started to laugh. But we became friends.

They appreciated the fact that there was a guy on the other end of the radio who cared about what was happening to them. After all, it's their only link with help if they get in trouble. If I don't hear from a unit for *an hour, I would call them. Not to break their balls, not to get them in trouble. To see if they're okay. The guys knew that. They could hear it in my voice.*

Some of these guys on Nine One One just did not give a shit. I'd see a guy not pick up his phone, let four or five calls pass when all the phones are ringing, and I'd yell, "Hey, you fucking asshole, start picking up some calls." When that didn't work, I'd throw my coffee cup. "Jerkoff, pick up the fucking phone."

We were supposed to be helping people.

That's all I could think about. This wasn't a game. These weren't just telephone calls. These were real people in real trouble. I remember one call, this lady says, "There's a man with a gun outside my door." I am talking to a woman who has a guy with a gun outside of her door. If I don't get her help, who will?

Bang, I start pushing units on it and I keep her on the phone. Meanwhile, I'm jumping out of my skin. I want to rush over and save this lady, but I gotta stay on the radio and move the units.

It can also break your heart. Somebody calls that their husband isn't breathing and you push the panic button—they literally have a button to get an ambulance immediately and it's called a panic button. And you stay on the phone to calm her down and the guy's dead. But you can be a comfort, you know? Even at the worst of times, a cop can be a real comfort.

Chapter 13

"You are married?"

"Married. Oh, yes, sir. We have two children. Richard and Jaclyn."

In 1969, I was working in construction when I met Regina. Or, rather, I was not working that day, which is what led to our meeting. See, it was raining. One of the cold, miserable rainy days in late fall. I was on the high steel at the World Trade Center. But when it rains, you can't work. It's too dangerous. You have to report in anyway, just in case it lets up.

Well, on this particular day, they closed the job down and I had the day off. I went into this coffee shop down on Rector Street down near Wall Street. I saw these two girls at a table and I went over and began to bother them. They didn't mind. They were giggling and enjoying themselves. I just walked over and opened my mouth.

"Hey, how are you doing, girls? My name is Bo."

They looked at each other like I'm weird. Usually I go for the blond and her friend was a blond. But I went for Regina. I was immediately attracted to her and I asked for her phone number but she wouldn't give it to me. She wanted to give it to me, but I guess she didn't want to look too eager. Her friend gave it to me.

There were a lot of very polite dates after that. Four years of dates. I would bring her flowers and candy because she was a very good girl. High moral standards and all that. Her family was very proper. Russian Jews from Far Rockaway. Her father had some furniture stores.

In any case, it was a long courtship. We went together for four years and we finally got married by a friend, Supreme Court Justice A. L. Lerner. Religion was not too big a thing with either of us. There was no pressure there. Not as far as I was concerned. Not any from my family, either. They liked her. They liked her better than they liked me. They considered me a bum, which I do not deny. I do not argue with that.

After we got married, we set up house. I taught Regina how to cook. I learned that from my father. She kept a nice home. She is a great mother and a very understanding wife. She has to be.

She says I'm a lousy husband. She says that I never should have got married. I can see her point. But I don't know how to help it. Listen, when you work the hours I work, it's not normal. Out for two, three, four days at a time. Hanging around bars with the guys. Come home to change clothes and kiss the kids and then go out again. It's hard on her. I can definitely see her point. But I don't know what I could do about it. Except maybe change my basic nature, which is not an easy thing to do.

"You entered the academy when?"

"It was the first class in 1972, sir. Company 72 A."

"Your academic standing was in the high nineties. And the physical?"

"Yes, sir, I won the physical fitness award. Rusty Staub of the New York Mets presented the plaque to me."

I did not like the academy. It was like going back to school and I did not like going to school. I hated sitting in a classroom and getting lectured. It's bullshit. I could see out the windows, which is where I wanted to be.

But I knew that it was only four months and I could handle four months. Half a day physical, half a day academic. I never studied. I could never crack a book. This is why I never tried for promotions in the book part of the job. I retained what I had to retain because I knew what would be important on the job. And, like I said, I did well in the academics.

During that time, I became a kind of class leader. I was outspoken. Put it this way—we would always have a little laugh when I was around. I brought a little humor into the seriousness of the academy.

The instructors liked me because I was good at the physical part. I'd do 150 push-ups, 30 pull-ups. Forty-one counted squat thrusts. Well, this goes back to high school when I was the Eastern Seaboard Marine Corps Physical Fitness Champion.

But the big thing with the instructors at the time, they were very worried about our safety. A lot of cops were getting killed in the line of duty and they made a very big point of how to protect yourself. Approach a car with your hand on your gun and your partner watching the other side. They were very emotional about it, because so many cops were being killed.

It was a military-like thing and we were divided up into companies. The training was broken down into phases and the important stage—the one that counted—was pistol training. After you went to the range and qualified to handle a pistol, that's when it started to feel like you were becoming a cop.

The most important turning point was the day they let you take the gun home. Until then, it was like going to Coney Island. They give you the gun, you shoot off your hundred rounds, then you give it back. But now it is ours. Now it is not in this controlled environment. Then you felt the power of having a gun.

We were riding back to Queens, four of us. We had the guns in our black bags. But we kept taking them out and looking. Could not stop looking, feeling them. Four young guys in a car on the Long Island Expressway fondling their pistols. It musta looked funny from the other cars.

When I got home, I went right to my room. My mother was in another room. I took the gun out of the bag and I held it. It felt like—I don't know, so much power. I remember looking around to see if anyone was watching. This is in my own room with the blinds closed. I found myself toying with it. Playing with it. Cocking it. Pushing it. Flashing it. Looking in the mirror to see how I looked with this thing in my hand. Loading it. You hear those neat mechanical clicks. Then—and I know this sounds strange—putting it in your mouth and taking it out.

It's some sort of psychological thing. You fuck with it. You're fucking with the gun, like saying, "I'm tougher than you, gun."

I talked to a million guys and they all do it. They don't like to admit it, but they all do the same fucking thing. They say, "Hey, you know, I did the same fucking thing." Cock it. Flash it around. Put it in your mouth, take it out, saying, "Look, I did that. I defeated the gun." It's like taking the magic away from the gun. Now the magic is mine.

After I did that, I never did it again. It was just something that I had to get out of my system, you know? Such power behind it. I had to overcome the power of that gun.

"Where did you take your field training?"
"The Seven Seven, sir."

The Seven Seven in Brooklyn was supposed to be a dumping ground. This is where they found all that corruption with cops stealing dope and selling it. Bergen Street. The field training is the last two weeks of the academy training, so you're still wearing the recruit uniform. They want you to have some knowledge of the job before they turn you loose. My first tour was a four-to-midnight.

"Dietl to Jones and Smith."

You're assigned to a pair of veterans and you ride around and answer radio calls. They tell you, "Kid, don't be too eager." And they tell you war stories, you know, showing off. And we get there and I'm riding with two old pros and we get a report to investigate something at a Spanish grocery on Buffalo Avenue. There's nothing there and we wind up sitting in the back of the bodega having a couple of beers, bullshitting with the owner.

This is a violation. These guys are neglecting their work. But this is a very busy precinct. A combat command. And you cannot appreciate the pressures that these cops worked under.

It's a funny thing about places like the Seven Seven: There is more comradeship there than in the quieter precincts. You hear a ten-thirteen in the Seven Seven, and there will be a response faster than anyplace else. I was in a Queens precinct and no one talked to each other. They were all alienated. Not the Seven Seven. These guys were all brothers. Like one big family.

These guys I ride with that first night were good. We're riding down the avenue and they spot a theft. Two guys stealing a radio from a car. I didn't spot it, but they did. They ride past and they don't say a word.

They pulled up behind and say, "Got a collar for you, kid."

These were real professional cops. They were cautious and had the situation under total control. At the time, I thought that they had twenty years on the job. But they'd only been on for four or five years. A busy precinct can make you a veteran in a hurry.

We'd walk down the street and they would point out things, things you wouldn't ordinarily notice at a quick glance. This guy's dealing heroin. Those guys in the doorway are junkies.

And then, we're riding, and suddenly, the guy stops the car, pulls over, and throws this guy up against the wall. He does a pat and finds a gun.

I could not believe it. How did he know the guy had a gun? The guy was wearing a loose shirt. It didn't match the pants and the shoes. And it looked like this guy was careful about how he matched his pants and his shoes.

The way a guy walks. Favoring a certain side. Not swinging an arm with the same free swing that moves his other arm. As if he's protecting something. A gun.

You get to know these things. You get to spot the peculiar traits of a guy packing an illegal gun. Not all of these things will stand up in a court. But a cop knows. A good cop can spot a wrong guy from the most insignificant little details.

Now, these guys were really nice. They gave me this collar, the gun collar. And that was a big one. You always like to take an illegal gun off the street because you figure it can be used against a cop. This is an important arrest.

There's all kinds of action in the precinct. We get a ten thirty-one—burglary in progress. An auto parts store. And we charge in there with our flashlights and guns out. We find a couple of guys hiding, buying a couple of couches.

It was exciting, but I am conscious of the danger. I go in in my combat crouch, with my nonshooting hand diagonally across my chest, protecting my heart, my vital organs. They impressed this on me at the academy. There's this one guy who was saved by this. He caught three in his arm. Made a vest out of his arm. This is before the bulletproof vests became popular.

I always had dreams. Recurring dreams. About being shot. I'd rather take it in the arm than the chest. That's something that's always stayed with me. The dreams.

Funny thing in the dreams—I'm shot, but I can't shoot back. My finger won't work the trigger. I'm not able to squeeze. It's always slow motion. There's someone coming at me with a gun. I can see him very clearly and I know that if I have my gun out, I'll be okay. Then I have my gun, but it won't shoot. I'm trying, but nothing is happening. I'd wake up and I'd be sweating. Regina would be there, looking scared. She said I screamed out loud about being shot, but I don't remember screaming. All I remember is trying to pull the trigger and nothing happening.

Chapter 14

There are things common to all members of the police department. The chiefs had all started as rookies. They had all spent a first day on a first assignment. They knew what that meant. They could guess what it felt like.

"Your first assignment was in Queens."

"That's right, Chief. The One Ten. Elmhurst."

"That's an active house, isn't it?"

"I would say moderate, sir."

It's an old house. Falling-down brick on Forty-third Avenue off Junction Boulevard. But it looked like a palace to me. Now I am a real cop.

My first assignment was on the neighborhood police team. Our mission is to keep the sector calm.

I'd ride with a bunch of different guys, all the time gaining experience, and I am beside myself. I love this.

One day, I am in the stationhouse and getting ready for roll call and these guys come in—long hair and beat-up jeans and beards. They looked great. They go right past the roll call and they go up to the squad room, like they owned the world.

"Who are those guys?" I asked my sergeant.

"Anti-Crime," he says.

Citywide Anti-Crime. That's what I wanted to be.

But right now I was a rookie and fighting my way to the top in the One Ten. So now I got a reason. I let everyone know I'm looking. Any arrest that comes along, I'll take it. A lot of these old hairbags don't want the bother of paperwork and going down to court. They don't even bother to answer the radio. You get in the car and they say, "Let 'em call you a couple of times."

Fuck you. We get a call, we go. I'll take anything. They didn't want me to drive the first half of the tour, figuring that's the busy part of the night. They want to drive the first and let me have the back half, when it's quiet. But that's bullshit and I roll.

One night, two weeks after I get into the precinct, they give me a recruit to ride with me. He looks at me like I'm an old pro. If he looked at my holster, he'd see the leather was as new as his. Well, this one night we handle about twenty-five jobs, until about six-thirty in the morning. Burglars, muggers, car thefts. Soup to nuts.

We're riding along and I did not know the boundaries of the precinct too well since I am pretty green. We're heading out toward Woodside and I see a gypsy cab parked at the curb on Skillman Avenue. It looks funny. This is a cool night and I see exhaust coming out of the car and I see some kind of motion. Like a fight in the back seat. So I tell the kid, "Let's check this out."

We move up on the car—he's on one side and I'm on

the other side—and we see this guy in the back seat. It looks like he's raping this blond girl. I pull open the door, I got my gun out, and I yell, "Police! Get the fuck out!"

The guy didn't stop. So, I put my gun back in the holster and I go in and I start to pull the guy off and he's got a knife in his hand. I grab the knife and we start wrestling. I punched the shit out of him in the car and the knife goes flying. And we start to handcuff this guy.

Meanwhile, the girl in the back seat is hysterical. She's screaming and crying. I got this guy cuffed and thrown up against the back of the cab, his pants down around his ankles, his dick hanging out. "You move and I'll blow your fucking brains out," I tell him. I get on the radio and I am so excited I forget the call sign. "This is one-ten Charlie," whatever, and the guy on the radio asks for my location and I look at the street sign. This is when I find out that I am outside the precinct. Four blocks.

Cars start piling in and they take the girl to Elmhurst General Hospital and I stay with this guy—a Jamaican.

This is my first jury trial and we lose. That piece of shit walks. He claimed that she was consenting, and she had one disorderly conduct arrest. But that wasn't why we lost. The reason we lost that case was that the kid and I didn't get our stories together. We didn't talk about it. Then we go into court and this smart defense lawyer starts tearing us apart. Finding little inconsistencies. Nothing crucial. Nothing that would make any real difference. Just technical shit that any normal human being might forget six months later.

They don't teach you this in the academy. How to get ready for court. You have to get your stories straight.

The small details. What time was it? What was your last job? What made you stop? What did you say? What did he say?

You learn fast on the job. I learned to get the stories straight, no matter what the fucking book says.

It wasn't long after that I got my first homicide. An old couple, in their eighties. Some push-in burglar got into their house and beat the shit out of the woman and the man. The old man died and we were the first car on the scene. We called an ambulance, but I knew he was dead. The old lady was crying:

"We gave him everything. Why did he have to do this?"

I remembered this poor old woman, with blood all over her, sitting there with her dead husband, waiting for the ambulance, asking me a question I could not answer: "Why did he do this to us?"

A few weeks later, I locked up a burglar, some guy terrorizing all of Woodside. Turned out to be the same fucking guy. His prints matched the prints in the old lady's apartment. Now I had him for murder. That felt good. That felt like a score was evened up.

After a month, they let us pair up with our own partners. I got a guy named Roy Zinkiewicz. Young guy. We went to the academy together. And when we hit the street, we were hot shit.

"Let's hit Elmhurst Avenue," I'd say. And off we'd go. We had the scumbag Colombian drug dealers there. The old cops were afraid to go down that street. But I'd say, "Hey, we're the fucking cops! We go where the fuck we want to go."

The Colombians learned not to fuck with us. We started making a lot of cocaine and gun arrests. On Elmhurst Avenue. It made the old-timers look bad.

They'd been patrolling that street for years and coming up blank. The average cop in the One Ten made two arrests a year. Total. I made sixteen my first month.

Me and Roy would park the car and hide and watch the street. We'd see who was dealing, who was packing a gun, who was working as a lookout. I'd have my uniform shirt off and walk around with a T-shirt.

I wasn't married at the time, so I would find a nice Colombian broad and talk some shit and find out about this and that. I'd take an hour off, go get laid, then go get the bad guys. That R & R would boost the old morale.

Now, these bad guys are not exactly easy. They threaten cops. These Colombians are a little crazy. They shoot at cop cars. They're not too afraid, either. These are some bad dudes.

However, I refuse to take any shit. So I start to fistfight with these guys. "You don't like cops, huh, you dumb motherfucker?" Pow! "I'm the police." And we're rolling around on the ground, punching the shit out of each other.

We were hurting their business. They yell out, "Scumbag," and throw bottles at the car when we rode by. So I'd stop the car and walk over. Roy would be back there watching for a gun. "Stay the fuck off the street," I'd say. "You do business on the street, we'll lock you up."

We kept Elmhurst Avenue and Roosevelt Avenue pretty clean. At least we keep it moving.

When I went on duty, word was passed along the street, "Bo is out."

I heard that they put out a contract on me. Somebody's gonna murder me because I'm hurting their business.

Now I am not the only target. This was the time

when the Black Liberation Army was going after police cars. They had fucking hand grenades. We got permission from headquarters to use our own cars, to go plainclothes and follow behind the sector cars. Guys were coming to work with pump shotguns, automatic rifles with banana clips. And nobody was saying anything because this was war. Cops were dying. This was serious shit.

It didn't stop me. We continued to go after the Colombians and Equadorians. We literally locked up hundreds. We'd be tearing back and forth to Central Booking at the One Twelve on Yellowstone Boulevard like a shuttle.

Roy would be stuck there doing the paperwork or in court and I would go out with a hairbag. "Well, your car got an arrest," he'd say, and I'd shoot back, "That ain't the end of the night. Roll." One guy reaches across and shuts off the ignition. I said, "Look, you don't have to do a fucking thing. You can sleep. I don't really give a flying fuck. But the car rolls. End of story."

Within a month, I got my first medal.

It was a gun collar. Some guy on 104th Street and Northern Boulevard. We got a call, man with a gun. So, we get there, and I see the bulge in his waist. I said, "You are under arrest," and he starts to run and I go after him. I bring him down with a tackle and I am holding him with a head scissors. My partner is an old-timer and he keeps saying, "The kid's crazy."

When we get to court, this old fuck testifies—testifies!—that this young buck, those are his words, "This young buck goes running after this man. I do not want to get involved in anything that day." This is what he tells the jury. This is what he swears to in court.

The judge was a nice old guy. He was amused by my lazy partner. Took it as a joke. But he is impressed by me. "Officer Dietl," he asks, "could you show the jury how you managed to bring down the suspect?"

I show him and the judge is saying, "Remarkable! Remarkable!" A letter is written and a medal is ordered.

The One Ten began to get some more young guys in it. We began to have a bunch of eager beavers on late tours and I would coordinate all the sectors. We had a fucking army, converging on the drug dealers, cleaning up the streets. I mean, it was like a military exercise.

"First," I would say, "we are going to have dinner," because I like to have a good dinner and because it enhances morale. "Sector A, you bring the hamburgers. Sector B, Kentucky Fried Chicken. Sector Charlie, pizza." Now, these store owners would never charge us for the food. Just, "Hey, Bo, we're making a bank drop around two o'clock in the morning, if you could keep an eye on us."

And, of course, we would, because that's our job. The food came for nothing. I never felt that was corrupt. To this day, this minute, I see nothing wrong with that. I would never take a dime, but a hamburger is okay.

Okay, so the night crews would load up on the food and we'd all meet at the park. I always preferred the midnight tours because there's less supervision. We'd be chowing down and I'd be getting them all fired up. "We're gonna kick some ass tonight." See, guys went one of two ways. They either became like me—crazed with ambition—or else they just wanted to put in their eight hours and go home. We had a hot crew. And there we are with our banquet at Flushing Meadow Park.

For recreation, we'd go rat hunting. They had a lot of rats around the lake and we felt like we were doing a service, shooting the rats, as well as having a little fun.

You really have to sneak up on them. You get a nice moving target. And there were bonuses. We'd get some rapists—guys pick off girls on the street and take them to the park, which was not safe now with these rat-hunting, hungry cops.

We also had a degenerate among us who would sneak up to a couple making out and peek in. He'd see a steamed window and just hang out and then bang on the window.

Finally, the sergeant got a complaint about us and we had to cut down.

Now the word was getting strong that someone is out to murder me. So we get a little aggressive. We have code names for each other. I'm Lead, Sector B is Zinc, Sector Charlie is Gold. And the air is filled with "Lead to Zinc to Gold to Silver, move to kickoff." We seal off a street and move down—four cops on each end. And we got gun and narcotics arrests. Lock up the whole fucking block for disorderly conduct.

I get this one guy, a tough guy, and I take off his cuffs. "You want to kill me? Come on, kill me."

It's just him and me and I did not lose. I don't care if they brought King Kong out of the zoo, I am never gonna lose because I am doing right. This is what I believe.

I started to feel responsible for my guys. We were all young cops, but I was like the mother hen. One of my guys gets hurt, I feel very responsible. I would take it very fucking personal. So I started to protect them. Now, these guys are not stupid. They realize that I am being overprotective.

It would be a tricky thing to tell a man of Bo's tender sensibilities that he is smothering you, acting like a uniformed Jewish mother on patrol. But it had to be done. Every time there was any danger, Bo had the protective habit of moving in first, pushing his brother officers out of harm's way. Not that there weren't times when he needed help. Not that he expected to be out there alone. However, the line officers who make up the rank and file of the New York City Police Department, who have a language of their own, found their own way to deliver the message to Bo.

We get a psycho call and roll. Two cars show up at this apartment and there's this guy sitting in a big armchair and looking at us like he does not give a shit. One of the women in the apartment is bleeding because this psycho hit her. And he is looking at me and smiling. I can see that he's big, even though he's sitting down. We got four cops, but I step forward and I tell this psycho in the armchair that he is under arrest. He starts to laugh. I hate it when they start to laugh. Makes me think that they are laughing at the uniform.

"You are under arrest, let's go," I tell him.

He says, "Go fuck yourself."

Wait a minute. Go fuck yourself? This is no way to talk to a duly sworn officer of the law. I don't know which I hate more—the laughing or the go-fuck-yourself.

"Excuse me, sir, you don't seem to understand. I am placing you under arrest."

"Go fuck yourself."

Okay. That's it. The man is under arrest. I pull him out of the chair and he starts pounding me. We're rolling around on the floor and this is going on and on. We're wrestling for ten minutes and it begins to dawn on me that there are three other cops in this room and I am the only one fighting Godzilla. When I look around,

I see these three other cops sitting down on the couch. They're watching, like they got front-row seats. This is a show.

"Fellas!" I yell.

They applaud.

Meanwhile, the psycho is landing some good shots. I don't know what's going on, but I wasn't playing anymore. I'm landing a few good shots, too. I wanted to hurt this son-of-a-bitch. I wanted to cuff him and get him to Elmhurst General Hospital.

Finally, I get him cuffed and the three cops on the couch are still sitting there with their fingers up their ass. I'm calling them every kind of scumbag. "Didn't you see? Why didn't you help me out?"

One of the guys gets up. "Well, Bo, we knew that you had the situation under control."

The psycho's bleeding. I'm bleeding. My shirt is torn to shreds. We both look like we just came out of a fucking blender.

"Under control? What are you, fucking morons? I coulda been killed!"

"Nah, we were right here."

They're leading him out.

"Besides, we get this call every night," says another, and they start laughing like maniacs.

Some joke.

Life in the streets of Elmhurst broke down along strict ethnic lines. There was a great influx of Asians in the seventies—refugees from war and oppression. The Spanish and Irish residents began to feel the pressure of change. And, as in all such fluid times, the level of tolerance fell. It was most apparent in the outbreak of teenage gang violence. Spanish gangs brushed against Chinese gangs and Irish gangs. They all had colorful names—the Savage Skulls, the Seven Immortals.

There was a church on Forty-third Avenue. Saint Bartholomew's. The police commissioner, Codd, lived down the block. He went to church there. And they were having big problems with the Irish gangs. They'd drink too much and wear their brass knuckles and their leather outfits and try to act tough. I'd pull the radio car right up there where they were hanging out and I'd get out and I'd talk to them. Hey, it wasn't too long before that I'd been the same kind of punk. I wouldn't lock anybody up for drinking beer. Pretty soon I got a reputation as a good guy.

One night, there was a confrontation. A real gang fight. Guns, knives, razors—whatever. The Irish gang and the Spanish gang were gonna meet in Flushing Meadow Park. Just like West Side Story.

Well, I heard about it and I got into the middle. I had all my units out there in the park and I put us between the two gangs. One of the Spanish guys didn't know me. He starts mouthing off. I tried to calm him down, but he was making a disturbance. He called me a motherfucker. I had to slap the shit out of him in front of all his friends. He thought I was gonna arrest him after that, but I didn't. Then I apologized for slapping him in the face. I said he shouldn't have called me a name, but that I was wrong for slapping him like that. He gave me a pair of brass knuckles, like a peace offering.

I was working the scooters—I always worked the scooters when my partner was off—and I see the commissioner on his way to church. I salute and he smiles at me. "How's that condition with the Savage Skulls?" he asks.

"All cleared up, sir," I say.

"I heard you did a nice job."

Few days later, I am driving the scooter and all of a sudden I see a guy with a sawed-off shotgun. Long hair, hippie type. My eyes bug out and I crash the scooter into a parked car. Just walking around carrying a shotgun. I leap off and pull my gun. "Police, police, freeze!" I yell. I'm into a crouch, I'm ready to shoot this fucking guy. And he goes, "Federal Fire Arms and Tobacco." He's undercover, covering the back of some fucking building; I'm ready to shoot my first person and it's another fucking cop.

I loved being on that scooter. You could really get involved. I'd ride down Eighty-second Street and I'd tell all the store owners, "Hey, you got any problems, you tell Bo." Everybody knew me. And I'd love taking the scooters to court. Get in and out of traffic, save a lot of gas. Pretty soon, everybody was taking the scooters to court. There'd be a fucking parade of cops on scooters down Yellowstone Boulevard going to Queens Criminal Court. Now, this one time, we are going down Queens Boulevard, passing Yellowstone Boulevard in the One Twelve Precinct. And all of a sudden, there's a gang war. There's about thirty of them and only me and another cop.

Trouble. They spot us and duck down into the subway. We go right down after them. This is serious. We pick up zip guns, chains, knives, real guns, knuckles—everything. We end up locking up eight of them. So we start getting some shit from the judge. "You were supposed to be here in court on this case." "Yeah, but we had a gang war. We got arrests."

And these assholes would say, "What do you mean you got arrests? You're supposed to be in court."

This was the same mentality that made me crazy on the job. I'd see these cops studying for the sergeant's test. They'd be parked in Flushing Meadow Park and a call would come over, robbery in progress, and they're still studying. One time a ten-thirteen comes over and I see this guy and he doesn't even lay down the book. A ten-thirteen! Another cop in trouble. I took my radio car and smashed it into the back of his cruiser. I yell over, "You cocksuckers, you got a ten-thirteen, you get your ass moving or I will personally rip off your nose." Some of these hairbags wound up as sergeants and lieutenants and captains.

It was a time when Bo Dietl dipped a toe into the waters of the job and found the temperature to his liking. He loved it. He loved it all. Not the assholes. Not the bureaucratic hassles. But the job. That he loved.

I didn't want to take days off. I never called in sick. I had this feeling—if I could arrest everybody doing every crime in New York, I would have done it. I was a psycho on a mission. It wasn't work. It was always changing. Always . . . fun!

There were odd moments. One night we get a call. An accident at Ninetieth Street and Roosevelt Avenue. This is a rainy night and an accident is not unusual. It's about two-thirty in the morning and the rain was like a motherfucker. We get there and there are four cars in a head-on collision. Four ways. What are the odds? Four cars hitting an intersection at the same instant from four different directions.

And every single one of them is drunk. There are four

people in every car—all drunk. Completely out of control. It's all in Spanish, so I do not understand a word.

I am pulling this one off someone, so another one jumps on and starts pounding away.

Now one guy had a cowboy hat on, so I take it. I put it on my head and I start yelling: "Hold it. This is marshal law. You are all under arrest."

I grab one guy and I handcuff him and we take them down to the One Twelve. They have to blow up the fucking balloon. We have to wait for the technician. I really feel sorry for these guys—four drunk drivers. So we buy them a couple of six-packs and they're drinking and waiting to blow up the balloon and I'm drinking with them and getting to like them. Having a few myself.

I'm telling Roy, "We never should have gotten involved, the paperwork is such torture. These guys are all illegal aliens and are going to get deported." Finally, the technician shows up and they blow up the balloons and they all register drunk and it occurs to me that my buying them the six-packs did not help them pass the test.

Now, in the summer of 1972, riots started breaking out in Jamaica. Somebody killed a kid and the streets are suddenly hot. We are assigned to the one-oh-three, where the riot is going on, and when we show up, they say, Okay, one-ten Boy, you are assigned to Engine Company Blah Blah Blah. All we had were these old scooter helmets, but it's better than nothing.

We show up at the firehouse and they break out some beer and we're sitting in the back laughing and joking. Firemen are great. Stand-up guys. Next thing, we get a call for a fire. Ding, ding, ding, here we go. We put on our helmets. We figure it's a bunch of bullshit. We're going down this road and there's a crowd of about a hundred people and we pull up in front of the fire. It was a car. Someone set it on fire. To draw the firemen. All of a sudden, Boom! A Molotov cocktail.

The firemen put it out, but there's a railroad trestle, concrete, and I see a flash. Before I heard the sound, I see the flash. Then, Pow! Pow! Pow!

One of the firemen yells, "They're shooting! Let's get the fuck out of here."

Roy dives into the front seat of the car. I'm out there on the street. I start shooting out the lamplights so they can't see us. I say, "C'mon, Roy." The guy that was shooting at us was in front of a crowd. I kept shooting over his head because I was afraid of hitting someone.

Roy gets out and starts shooting the lamplights. The bullets are hitting around me and we are shooting at the fucking lamplights like a pair of morons. The firemen are yelling, "Get the fuck out of there!" I ended up firing every bullet I had at lamplights. Then I grab my nightstick and I am ready to run into the crowd, to grab the guy with the gun.

Roy is on the radio: "Ten-thirteen! Ten-thirteen! South Road. Officers under fire."

I was enjoying the fuck out of it. I am running around like I am in heaven. The only reason I left is because I ran out of bullets.

We get back to the engine company firehouse and there are bullet holes in the fire engine. There are bullet holes in the sector car. And I was thrilled. The firemen are in awe.

"You are one crazy person," said one fire lieutenant.

Chapter 15

"You volunteered for Anti-Crime."

"I did."

"Why?"

"I believe that it suited my abilities, sir. I had an aptitude for the work."

When I was in the academy, I got a piece of advice from one of the better instructors. He told me, "Work hard that first year. Don't get sloppy or lazy or, worse, corrupt. Work harder than you have to work and the whole world will open up for you."

Not that anybody had to tell me to work hard. I always worked hard. I wanted to better myself. I even went to school. Took some credits at the John Jay College of Morons and Assholes. But I couldn't take the classroom bullshit seriously. I am listening to people talk about the theory of how people turn to crime because they are underprivileged. About the norm of their conditions. And I am the only white guy there and I am clearly a cop and I am saying: No, no, no, this isn't the way it has to work. I have seen people grow up poor and not turn bad. Bad is bad. They think I'm a racist and they know I'm a cop, so no one listens to me.

Besides, I am learning more out on the street than in this classroom where this professor thinks I am one step short of an ape. It was pure book bullshit.

This professor had no idea of what I was talking about. He thought evil was some social problem, that it was always somebody else's fault. I thought it had something to do with the guy who commits the crime. In any case, I never did a term paper and after a while, I just stopped going. And I still got a B.

Meanwhile, I am tearing up Queens, running pushers off the fucking street. And this is not theoretical bullshit. After a little more than a year, I was called down for an interview with the Citywide Anti-Crime Unit—the unit that ran the undercover decoys and plainclothes operations. The headquarters was located on Randall's Island, beneath the Triborough Bridge. The Bat Cave.

Now, I had no "hook," no angle, no special access, which seemed to be a prerequisite. Everybody else had some kind of a "hook." But I did have 150 arrests in a year.

There was a lieutenant and two sergeants. They talked about arrests and life in general, but it was all leading up to one question:

"Would you consider decoying?"

"I would fucking love it, sir."

"Wait a second. Hold on, Officer Dietl. Do you know what it is to decoy?"

"I believe so."

"It is not what you think. You put on a disguise. You get all made up and you try to have people rob you. This is not an easy thing. This is very dangerous."

He is telling me all the bad points, one by one, and I am just sitting there saying to myself, Yeah, yeah, tell me more.

See, I actually had a taste of this. Back in the One Ten, they were having this major problem with drugs. Could not cope. The fucking Seventeenth Division was overrun. So they grab a few of the younger-looking guys—and I had this baby face—and I go out on this buy-and-bust program. And I love it. I'm going out in civilian clothes, in my own car, and I'm running down drug locations. I was locking up and marking dealers, and then the narcotics guys come in and make the busts.

I see in this that I am good out on my own. I know how to operate. I know how to work without close supervision. And I enjoy the freedom. The autonomy.

The narcotics people asked me if I wanted to go into that, but it didn't really interest me. I just never thought that drugs was the real problem. It doesn't seem any worse than alcohol. A victimless crime. Besides, I just got out of Ozone Park and half my friends were on dope. I always believed that it should be decriminalized.

I wanted Citywide Anti-Crime. This was my pick. This is combat. The real heavy hitters.

It took four months and I called every day. See, again, I told everybody that I was going into Citywide Anti-Crime and when it didn't come down right away, I felt like a jerk. That was my problem: I told other people. To me it wasn't exciting unless other people knew. Half the pleasure is telling your friends.

By the fall of 1973, they called me down again and I was in.

One of my first anti-crime decoy partners—God, you should have seen him—was Pete Mantovi. Beautiful guy. I looked at him and thought he was gay. Six-foot-three and dressed like a movie star. He had polished fingernails.

Pete was an aristocrat. He'd show up at the Two Five with a brace of pheasant that he'd shot on Randall's Island. Then he'd cook them. Oh, he was some cook. The anti-crime unit in East Harlem dined on pheasant under glass. With the correct wine. Pete knew about wine.

But the man had eighteen years on the job and he never made an arrest.

"Who's gonna try?" I tell him, after we go out night after night and come up blank. "You're six-foot-three and you look like Cary Fucking Grant! Who's gonna be dumb enough to try you?"

So I take him down to an army-navy store and I outfit him with coveralls and workshirts and painter's hats. I hide all that surgically cut hair under a hat. I roll dirt all over him and he finally begins to look like shit. Well, not shit, but at least he doesn't attract a crowd with his good looks.

So I make him my backup. The man cannot be a decoy, not in a million years, because even with the best Hollywood makeup, he still looks good. But he can stand down the street and look out for me. He turns out to be a great backup. All that polish, and he'd dive through a wall to save me.

Now we are running decoys all over the city and it is working great. First collar is mine. Next is Pete's. Then

135

we go down the list—who needs a collar? That's how we work in anti-crime. We look out for each other. It's a very tight brotherhood.

One night, right after New Year, January 6, 1977, we're working Forty-second Street and Seventh Avenue, which is scuzz headquarters of the world. Pete's sitting in the van we use to lock up our prisoners and I'm on the steps leading to the subway. All of a sudden, along comes this wolf pack, real wise-ass bastards. The girl looks me over and says in Spanish, "He's got a wallet."

I was wearing a seersucker suit and one of the guys just comes over and breaks a beer bottle over my head. No warning. Bam! I wasn't wearing a hat or anything so I am momentarily stunned.

The girl begins to swing away at me, tearing up my suit. She was a fucking savage. She clawed up my whole face with her nails. I end up clocking her. After that, she goes for my eyes. I turn around, and, I don't hit her with my fist, I slap her across the face. It knocks her over. We finally get her cuffed, along with the guys, and we handcuff them to the back seat. Five prisoners.

So now we're going back to Midtown Precinct, going downtown on Seventh Avenue, and we pull up at a light at Thirty-fifth Street. We're next to a taxi and I look down and I see that the cabdriver has a 9-millimeter pistol on the front seat of the cab. I get out and I flip my badge and I say, "Police." I do not get my gun out right away and I open the driver's door. Now the guy's window is open—it's important that you picture the open window on the driver's side.

I open the car door with my left hand. And the guy floors the cab. My arm got hooked on the window. I have one foot on the floorboard of the car, one arm hooked in the open window. And the door is swinging wide open.

By now I have my gun out in my right hand and the guy takes out a blackjack from under the front seat and starts beating my arm. He's got the thing floored and he's trying to beat me off the car.

Pete is in the van with the prisoners, chasing me down Seventh Avenue. He's on the radio, he's blowing his horn, and I am holding on for all I'm worth. The guy's beating me with the fucking blackjack and I'm swinging at him with the fucking gun.

I start to plead. "Stop the car," I beg. "I swear I won't lock you up! Just stop the car and I'll let you go."

He knows I'm full of shit and I know if I fall off I'm fucking history. We are really moving down Seventh Avenue. Tires screeching. Civilians screaming. Pete blowing his fucking horn. Me trying to talk this fuck into sparing my life.

Pete is trying to cut the guy off with the van, but it's hard. He's got me out there, swinging on the door, so he's got to be careful. By now I'm crazed. When Pete gets close, I yell, "Hit him!"

It would kill me, but I didn't give a shit. I wanted this fuck dead. "Hit him!" I'm screaming to Pete. "Kill the fuck!"

At the same time, I'm beating him with the fucking gun. I was getting better shots at him because he was sitting back and he wasn't able to move as much as I was. He had to drive and all I had to do was swing. I break his fucking nose.

Finally, twenty blocks later, he piles into a lamppost. I'm thrown in the street, bleeding and cut to shit. The other cops see me laying there and they think I'm dead. I'm bleeding from the decoy in Times Square, I'm bleeding from the cabdriver, I'm bleeding from flying in the gutter. I look like I should be in intensive care or the morgue.

But then I start to crawl back in the gutter. Pete doesn't know what to make of it. "Where the fuck do you think you're going?" he asks me.

I grunt. I can't make any real noise, just sounds. All I know is that I want to eat that cabbie's fucking eyeballs.

The other cops are watching, they don't know whether to laugh or cry. Finally, Pete stops me. They throw me in the back of a police car and take me to the hospital. Turns out that this cabdriver had warrants out for him all over the place.

At the hospital the doctors took X rays—everybody thought I had to have a thousand fractures. The doctor comes in and says, "I don't think I've ever seen a skull this thick." Only a concussion. So, they patched me up and let me go. They were getting to know me there. A regular customer.

But you can't let fear destroy you. I remember the first time I was conscious that someone wanted to kill me. This was in '74 and I was on decoy up at the old Manhattan Hotel on Forty-fourth Street and Eighth Avenue. Some guy comes up to me and puts a knife in my side. I turn around and we had a fallout fight and I realize that he's trying to cut me. He's got his knife and he's trying to use it. I had to pull my gun. I locked him up, but I went right back out again. You can't let these things get to you.

The next night, after the incident with the cabdriver, I was back out again.

There was a time when I actually thought of becoming an instructor. They didn't have many young guys out there and I thought maybe I could teach them something. Because you really have to know what you're doing. One of the decoys got his throat slashed, ear to *ear. That's when you realize, hey, this is serious shit. After that, I would hunch up my back so they wouldn't get a clean shot at my neck.*

Very scary. One night, I'm out there in Times Square and this guy comes along. He escaped from jail. He was doing time for homicide. I could see there was something crazy about him. Then I spotted the butcher knife. So I come out of the decoy and I say, "Police."

The guy pulls the knife. The lieutenant and the other backups are across the street and this guy is slashing away, trying to cut me. The lieutenant is yelling, "Shoot him, Bo! Shoot the son-of-a-bitch!" And I am up against a wall and I take my gun out, but I know that I am not going to shoot this guy. I keep moving sideways. Jumping away. I go about a quarter of the way down the block and I yell, "Jump him, Johnny!" There's no Johnny there and I go to grab him and he cut my hand wide open. I take the knife away and I manage to cuff him. This is no fucking game.

But I couldn't shoot him. The guy was a psycho.

The lieutenant is pissed. Really pissed. "What's wrong with you? Why didn't you shoot him?"

"I don't know," I said. "I figured I could handle it."

And I am bleeding all over the street.

There are things about it that I cannot explain. The drive. The desire. I can't let a thief get away.

Lots of times squatting in a doorway on decoy the legs go to sleep on you. You're supposed to hold up your arm for the backup to move in, but they can be far away. So, one night, a guy puts a gun in my side and says, "Don't move." He takes the wallet and I see that the backup is useless. I try to get up, but three hours out there and my legs are gone. So I jump on the hood of a cab and we go after the guy. The cab catches up with him, but he stops short and I go flying. I'm laying there in the gutter again, maybe dead, who knows?

The cops have the prisoner at gunpoint, but somehow, he gets away. He starts running. I see this and even though I'm laying in my own blood, I get up and I go after him. I make a flying tackle and then I pass out.

I began to pile up overtime now. I am working a lot of shifts and I go down to court and I have to wait for my cases and all this is overtime. Meanwhile, it is very boring to wait in court so I go across the street to Maruffi's Bar and I watch TV and I drink shaker glasses full of ice and Johnny Walker Black. The court officers call me when my case comes up, and, as a professional courtesy, I would buy them drinks.

I had a tremendous capacity for drinking at this time. I could drink a quart and a half of whiskey and still walk a straight line. And I had a tremendous capacity to bounce back. Four hours' sleep and I'm fine again.

Now, Maruffi's had a lot of cops coming in there drinking. Some of these guys are real amateurs. So, one day, I am down in the basement john and some drunken cop comes pounding on the door. "Oh, Bo, let me in, let me in!" I yell back: "Fuck off." Then, Bing! a round comes through the door. It hits the sink and ricochets away. But it was very scary.

I go up and the guy is at the bar and I pick him up and throw him across the fucking bar. "I'm sorry, I'm sorry," he's crying. "The gun just went off."

Some of these assholes didn't know what they were doing when they were drinking.

Meanwhile, I am beginning to build this reputation as an arm-wrestling champion. Everyone comes in to Maruffi's to try me out. And no one can beat me. The *funny thing is, when I get a few drinks in me, I'm even stronger. No cop ever beat me.*

They did set me up and beat me once, however. They got a guy who was the Eastern Super Heavyweight Arm-wrestling Champion—a professional. They sneak him in as a ringer at the Castle Harbor Casino in the Bronx while we are having a police function. Two hundred and fifty cops. So they bring this fucking ape in and he beat me. But he didn't beat me fair. First of all, I walked into it cold. I didn't have a drink. Second, he's not even a cop.

So, anyway, I am feeling very bad about losing my title. They had two girls there and they did a strip on top of three tables. Afterward, they were looking for volunteers to take on the two girls. One young guy goes up, but he couldn't get it up. I'm sitting there, feeling a little defeated, so I jump up and all the time I'm screwing the two broads, I am staring at the inspector who has been a real supporter. Inspector Grunwald. He liked me.

"There is this business on your record about attacking an assistant district attorney."

"No, sir, I did not attack an assistant district attorney."

"A female assistant district attorney."

"We had words."

"Words?"

"This female assistant district attorney tried to shit-can one of my decoy arrests. This was a case in which a suspect hit me over the head with a beer bottle. She wanted to knock it down to a violation. There was a female who attacked me and cut me up pretty bad and this female district attorney said, 'Oh, it's only another decoy, give her a disorderly conduct.'

I got angry, sir, and said, 'This was an out-and-out robbery.'"

"Was that the extent of it?"

"Not quite. I told her a little about decoy work and she did not appear to be sympathetic. She insisted on knocking the case down. So I said, 'I hope that the guy you turn loose robs you.'"

"The complaint is in your record."

"With all due respect, I consider it line of duty."

In 1975, with a lot of other good cops, I got laid off. Because of the budget crisis. There were five thousand cops laid off. The next day, there is a big demonstration and laid-off cops march across the Brooklyn Bridge and I am there wearing my rack of forty medals. The most decorated cop to be laid off. They did interviews with me and Muggable Mary on all the news shows—she got laid off, too.

Some of the cops were drunk and they started getting into fights with some of the bosses. I pulled a few off. I started to talk to the guys. Calming them down. "This won't do any good," I said.

Three days later, I am reinstated.

Chapter 16

The superchiefs who interviewed him in the spring of
1982 didn't know it, but something had broken in Bo
Dietl after the layoffs. It didn't show up in the bare
record. Bo's work in the field was still unmatched. But
that soft core of innocence that seemed to propel him
was turning cold and brittle. He was growing a hard
kernel of doubt. They did it once. They could do it
again.

It wasn't only the layoffs with their deep reminder
that civil service was not the safe, solid bunker he
imagined. Life had taken some cruel turns for Bo.
Since 1978, the happy, outgoing nature was not quite
so rampant.

We had a tragedy in the family.

Bo's parents, Frank and Sally Dietl, actually had
two sets of children. First they had Frank junior and
then Carol. It was almost ten years until Alan came

along, and then another two years later came Bo—
Richard—the youngest.

By the time Bo was growing up, Frank and Carol
were out of the house and on their own. Frank was an
engineer and Carol was working as an executive
secretary. Bo knew Frank and Carol in a distant way.
Still, they were family, and to Bo, that is a sacred
relationship. Although he was closest to Alan, Carol
had to be protected and Frank always carried the
authority of the oldest brother.

There is still no absolute clarity about what happened. It is one of those terrible family shocks in
which everyone agrees not to talk too much about it.
The subject is too shattering, too threatening to bear
close examination. A deal has been made for silence.

*Three years after the layoffs, my daughter Jaclyn was
just born. This is how I date it. She was a month old. So
it is early May of 1978.*

*Frank had been living out on Long Island and one
day he just got tired of the rat race and he sold
everything and moved up to Vermont. He wanted a
better life for his kids. Frank and Marilyn had five kids.
I mean, he looks around and he sees the drugs and the
crime and he got fed up. Who can blame him?*

*They moved to Vermont and opened a Carvel in
Burlington.*

*To protect the kids, to escape the temptations. There
was Debra, the oldest. Then Judy and Bobby and Dawn
Marie and Kim. My brother wanted a better life. It's
very tough with five kids.*

*My niece Judy was the sweetheart of the family. She
had long blond hair—she was voted the prettiest girl in
school. She never even dated boys. She was very close to
the Italian side of the family. My mother loved that*

girl. You didn't have to tell Judy to get up and help with the dishes. And she'd always help with the cooking. She was everybody's favorite.

She was nineteen when they moved to Vermont and she decided that she wanted to go to college in Boston. "Fine," my brother says. "You want to go to college, that's great." It might be tough on the budget, but they'd sacrifice.

She was away at school for a while and my sister-in-law Marilyn, Frank's wife, heard some very disturbing rumors. Someone said that they saw Judy hanging out on the Combat Zone in Boston. The Combat Zone is where all the addicts and hookers hang.

Marilyn didn't tell Frank because he had a bad temper. Always yelling and threatening. She thought, Maybe, please God, it's a mistake.

But she heard it again. From someone else. It seems that Judy had met this black guy, Damian, and he was a pimp and Judy was involved with him.

First thing, Marilyn jumps on a bus and goes to Boston and takes Judy out of school. She brings her home. Meanwhile, this pimp, Damian, keeps calling my sister-in-law and asking to speak to Judy. Marilyn just hangs up on him and she keeps it from Frank because he will sure as hell go down to Boston and kill this fuck.

Nobody tells me, either, because if Frank is bad, I am worse. For example, when Carol was having problems with her husband, when he slapped her, I showed up at his door the next morning. I grabbed him by the shirt and I said, "If you ever touch my sister again I'll kill you."

The guy was shocked to see me. My sister was shocked to see me. They lived in California. But I didn't give a shit. When I heard that he slapped her, I *just hopped on a plane. So nobody tells me what's going on because I can be a little impulsive.*

Marilyn has this whole thing to herself. Judy is getting ready to go back to school. But Marilyn knows that she is really going back to this pimp.

This Damian is sending Judy letters. He had really turned her head. Bought her clothes. Took her to expensive places. She never did anything like that. She was a small-town girl.

The day before Judy is supposed to go back to school, she goes out with Marilyn to help her on the route. They had a station wagon and they used to deliver ice cream to churches and stores.

They were making a delivery to a synagogue and the door was locked. Marilyn told Judy to try the back. Marilyn had one of my brother's .38s. She had loaded it and brought it along.

Judy tries the door and it's locked. She turns and starts to walk back to her mother. Marilyn takes out the gun, she remembers that much. She takes out the gun and she kills her own daughter.

It was about eight-thirty at night and I'm working a six-to-two in the Two Five anti-crime unit. I get a call from the Burlington police.

"Officer Dietl?"

"Yes."

"There's been an accident. Your niece has been shot."

I called Alan and I said, "I'm making the next plane." He drove in and met me at the airport. We're flying up and I'm saying, "Oh, God, what could have happened?"

Of course, Alan knew a little bit about Judy and this pimp. But he doesn't say anything. I'm looking out the

*window and praying. "They didn't say she was dead.
They said she'd been shot. But they didn't say that she
was dead. They would have said something if she'd
been dead. Please, God, let Judy be all right."*

*We get to Vermont and we're met by a couple of
detectives. They introduce themselves. Then they say,
"We're going to ask you to do something. We have your
sister-in-law in the police station—"*

"How is Judy?"

"I'm afraid she's dead."

"Oh, Christ! Oh, Lord."

*"Officer Dietl, we need your help. We have your
sister-in-law in the station—"*

"What's she got to do with this?"

*"This is a very preliminary stage of the investigation,
Officer Dietl, and we do not know what happened. She
won't talk to her husband. She won't talk to us. She'll
only talk to you."*

*Well, as it turned out, she wasn't at the police station.
She was at the hospital. She was in a private room and
they put us in there together.*

"Marilyn, what happened?" I asked.

"Just close the door and I'll tell you."

*Then the floodgates open. She pours out this story,
the whole thing about what's been eating at her for
months and months. She is ranting a little—I've seen
that before—saying that she brought her daughter into
this world and she's not going to allow her to become a
junkie or a prostitute and she'll take her out of the
world first. She has a right.*

When people get on a jag like that, you let them go.

*She sits down and her hands are clasped together and
she can't look me in the eye. She says that when she
woke up that morning she heard a voice. The voice
said, "This is the day Judy dies."*

Oh, God, I am listening to things not even a priest should hear. I do not want to hear the things that she is telling me.

"I knew what I was going to do. I loaded the gun in the bedroom. Frank keeps it unloaded. I took Judy out on the route. I sent her to the locked door. I saw her walking back and I looked into her eyes. I looked straight into her eyes, Richie. Judy saw the gun and she saw the look in my eyes. She said, 'No, Mommy, no, Mommy!'

"I don't remember pulling the trigger. I just remember the hole hitting her chest."

She's telling me this like I'm supposed to handle it. This woman, who is supposed to be the godmother of my daughter, Jaclyn, only she never got to be the godmother because Jaclyn was just born.

She tells me this. She's describing this. And I am supposed to listen.

My first reaction was to want to go down to Boston and find this fuck and kill him. Execute him. I had a picture of him. I had spoken to some Boston cops who assured me that we could find him. No problem. Who's going to miss a pimp named Damian?

Finally, I say to myself, What is that going to accomplish? Then this pimp wins double. He wipes out the whole family. I can't do this to my mother.

Well, I ended up staying up there for two weeks. Me and Alan and Frank. I kept it from my mother and father. Although they found out. I don't know how, but my mother knows. She always used to ask about Judy. She always went on about how beautiful and how smart Judy was. But she never asked about her after this. Not after this happened. My father had just had a *stroke when this happened. My mother had one right afterward. Because she knew.*

My sister-in-law was convicted of murder in the second degree for killing Judy. She went to jail for two and a half years.

Frank visited her. When she got out of prison, they tried to live together. But I suppose that this thing is impossible to deal with. There are too many accusations. Too many recriminations. Too many things to deal with.

They moved to Texas and tried to put it behind them. But they couldn't and they got a divorce. He went his way and she went hers. But that didn't work either. The pain of being apart was worse than the pain of being together. After a few years, they remarried. They're together again now.

But there's no family gathering, no dinner, no occasion when that heaviness isn't felt. Every time I go to one, I see people looking off somewhere, as if Judy will come walking in.

The chiefs would credit the increase in pimp arrests after the spring of 1978 to Bo's resolute nature. He was always zealous, but now he seemed possessed.

I worked Times Square and I would see the kids, the runaways, and I'd see the pimps and it became a crusade. There wasn't a pimp who could walk on the same side of the street with me. I was a crazy man.

And on decoy, the ones I loved best were the ones in their three-piece suits. When I had a pimp rob me, when they'd pick my wallet, I'd love it. I used to get thrills up and down my body when they started going after the wallet. I wouldn't come out with my gun. I'd act like an idiot.

"Hey, that's my wallet," I'd say innocently.

And they'd say, "Just be fucking quiet."

"Please, please," I'd whine, "that's my wallet. You've got to give me back my wallet."

And the guy would say, "Quiet, fool."

"But, sir, can't I have my wallet back?"

"Go fuck your mother."

I would say, "That's not nice. You don't even know my mother."

I'd let them think they could beat me up. I wouldn't tell him I was a cop. And finally, like they all did, he would take a swing at me. I'd love when they'd take a swing at me.

He'd have one of those furry hats on. Real expensive. Real peacock hat. It was one of my biggest thrills to rip the hat to shreds. Then I would destroy those expensive three-piece suits. Real expensive. Pride-and-joy suits. I'd take the fucking pocket and rip it down. I'd rip the sides and sleeves. They'd come into the precinct house looking like Davy Crockett.

They would not know what hit them.

We were on decoy duty in Bryant Park and all of a sudden a ten-thirteen comes over the air. We run over and find one of the cops down. He had a heart attack fighting the pimps. There are the two pimps in their kelly green suits and they're standing there like two cocky birds, like the coolest things that ever walked the face of the earth. They got grins on their faces because they put a cop in intensive care.

Now I'm still in my decoy outfit—scars and blood all over my face.

"Put me in a cell with these guys," I tell one of the detectives. "When you get them in the stationhouse, put me in the cell."

They put me in the cell and I stumble and one of the pimps bumps me. I don't say anything. He pushes me away, wiping his hands, like I'm a skell and I'm gonna get him all nasty. There's one chair in the pen and the other pimp is sitting on it.

"Excuse me," I say, "but you're sitting on my chair."

"What's that, you white piece of shit? You scumbag."

"Me? Are you talking to me? Get the fuck off that chair."

He takes a poke at me and I lift him up and throw him across the fucking cell. The other one turns and, Boom! The ax comes down on him. I start taking his face apart. I also take apart his kelly green suit, which is his business office.

The three of us are all over the floor and the kelly green suits are getting all this red blood on them. I rip the suits. I rip the vests. They do not look like slick dudes anymore.

Meanwhile, I don't realize it, but not everyone got the word. There's another detective in another room. He sees the fight going on and he doesn't know that it's me. Actually, he's drunk. So he goes charging in, beating me with a fucking blackjack.

The other cops have to pull him off and I am half knocked out. He looks down at me and it begins to dawn on him.

"Bo," he says through his stupor, "is that you?"

They held a retirement party for the blackjack that knocked Bo silly. There was a cake and an official-looking paper putting the blackjack on three-quarters retirement pay. It was a time in which Bo and his cronies looked for any excuse for a party. Overtime was plentiful for the men working decoy. And so was crime. Life was a happy war between good and evil.

Going out into Times Square was like going out on the first day of the trout season. You tossed a line into the water and you came up with something every time. Every loser in the city hung out there. We took a survey once. The people we were pulling in had an average of 9.2 prior arrests. These were not innocent people being entrapped. We were getting bad dudes.

One guy, I remember, robbed me and I turned around and he starts running very fast. I go after him and this guy is quick. He's going over car tops, knocking people over. We had nine cops after this one guy and he is leaving us in the dust. Finally, he bumped into someone and he slows down a little and we catch him. Turns out to be an Argentinian soccer player. A professional. Boy, he was fast.

Some nights the seersucker suit would really take a beating. You have to buy your own clothes in decoy. So you try not to spend a lot of money. And you try to take care of it. You also wear your own rings and show your own wallet. Gives you an incentive not to get robbed.

There was one night at Madison Square Garden where eight guys attacked me. A pack.

I was out there and I heard them coming. First two of them. They shook me to see if I was awake. Then the others came along. I could hear them. They had that shuffle. A certain walk I could identify. Meant that they were out to rob someone. I called it the 155.30 shuffle. One fifty-five thirty is grand larceny under the penal code.

So, it turns out, a total of eight of them hit me. Bang!

I was just rolling along with them, letting them take whatever they wanted. Everything. I forgot I had my good ring in my pocket when I went out there to set up the decoy. I usually wore a fake watch and had a phony wallet. I put my real ring in my pocket. It was a beauty. Jade and gold with Chinese lettering. But this whole gang hit me and they were all over me and they got the real ring out of my pocket. That was the only thing upsetting to me.

So that's when I grabbed them. Eight of them and I grabbed four. The other four got away. They can mess with the phony stuff, but this was personal. I told the judge I would make a deal and reduce the charges to get back my ring. But I never did. It's still out there— somewhere.

The other outfit I had was a bum outfit. A ski hat on my head. You could pile that up and when they hit you, it could cushion the blow. You'd nail a bunch of bad guys then go into the van and change into the bum outfit because by now they made you.

Then you'd curl up or go into the mean lean. Lean in a doorway like a junkie in suspended animation. For hours. Man, I developed real strength in my legs. I could squat with a thousand pounds, I had such muscles. I worked at it. I had the best pickpockets in the world try to lift my wallet. But I had an educated ass. I could always feel the hand go in.

Miserable way to live. Some nights I was out there and the windchill factor was five below zero and I could feel the frostbite in my hands. But I was determined. I was not going out there without making an arrest. There were bad guys in the night and I was gonna get them. If I came up dry, if I didn't make an arrest, I felt defeated.

Maybe the worst thing about it is that you begin to

get cynical. Some good citizen comes along and tries to help you. Tries to lift you up and see if you're all right, and you think, This is a good guy trying to help his fellow man, and then this Good Samaritan tries to lift your wallet. We actually had a priest lift one of our wallets. He said he was trying to protect the guy, but he wasn't. The priest was a thief.

Chapter 17

"You think you're above the law, don't you?"

"No, sir."

"But you believe that the law is soft?"

"I don't know what you mean by soft."

"Let me put it this way, Officer Dietl: Isn't it your belief that the courts are lenient? That they turn loose dangerous criminals?"

"Isn't that your belief, too, Chief, meaning no disrespect?"

"I don't take the law into my own hands."

It was a big thing, going out on decoy in Harlem. Nobody wanted to do it. It was considered too dangerous. Listen, I didn't give a shit. It was decoy. One shitheel was the same as the next. I wasn't prejudiced. I used a theatrical-base makeup when I went out. It didn't exactly make me look black, but it made me look not quite so white. I got it in some makeup place in the theater district. Put it all over my face and hands and up my arms. In the summer, it itched like a motherfucker. In the heat, when you're waiting out there for hours, not moving a muscle, all you wanted to do was scratch. Just rake my fucking nails down the side of my face. In the winter, it felt like it was going to chap right off your face, along with an inch of skin. But it did the job.

And, it was all part of it.

Going out on decoy was a real ritual. All alone with a mirror and my makeup kit, putting my shit on. Getting my head together. You have to be pumped for that. You have to be ready.

First, I'd get that makeup all over my skin. Then I'd close my right eye with a Curad. Plant a scar over my left eye, caked with some Number Three blood around it. Took me an hour to get it right. Getting it perfect. Looking into the mirror, smiling, looked like a piece of shit.

There was nothing but fences and blown-out empty lots on Third Avenue, just above 125th Street on a summer night in 1979. No place to hide. Tommy looked around for a blind, a hallway. A hallway was his natural home while I was on decoy. It gave him a standing start and a view of the street, kept me in sight, gave him some shadows. Backups live in the shadows.

But there were no shadows, only the empty shit.

I was near 126th Street, leaning against a wall. I got my head down in that weird angle that only a drunk or a junkie could hold. I could see out of a corner, Tommy finally found a box spring out on the side street, some office equipment for the hookers. He dragged it over to the corner of a building, piled some garbage around it, *like he was building a bunker. Then he crawled inside and pulled the garbage in around the opening. The man could have been a Vietcong. You could come walking in from any angle and all you would see was garbage.*

It was dark and hot—must've been hotter under the box spring. We were out there for an hour and a half. I was a living statue, like those guys who advertise banks downtown.

Tommy saw them first. There were three of them. He was pretty sure he recognized one. Someone from Queens. What was it? Oh, yeah, he remembered. The guy skated a couple of times on armed robbery and carrying. He used a .45, if it was the same guy, the one from Queens. The two guys with him were barracudas riding along with the shark. Big. Healthy. Dangerous.

They made a pass, talking to themselves, laughing. Pretending that they didn't notice Bo slumped over against the wall. They were almost up to Tommy, walking slowly.

I could hear them going by, even though I was down into my thing. I didn't have to look up. Just hear the footsteps. Slow. Deliberate. Watching. Feet with eyes. Doing the 155.30 grand larceny walk. Very cool. Slow down to check out the chump. Then keep on going. Moving without moving. Nothing incriminating in a slow stroll around the neighborhood.

But the hair on my neck stood up. I could tell. My legs hurt like fuck from leaning so hard up against the wall. Was there enough blood still going around to move when the time came? They were almost on top of Tommy.

He could hear the guy from Queens. They stopped right by his box spring. "Fucked-up guy," he said. "That man got off at the wrong station."

Another one—one of the barracudas—spoke. "That look like a wallet in his pocket?"

"Maybe we should go back and discuss it with him," replied the man from Queens.

Tommy could see them now looking up and down the street, checking the area for traps; then they started back toward Bo—a purposeful, silent march. One of the young ones stopped. "Hold on, man, be right with you. I gotta take a leak."

He came back and began pissing on Tommy's box spring. It goes with the territory, thought Tommy grimly.

Meanwhile, the other two approached Bo. "My man, you feelin' okay?" asked one. "You don't look so good."

The second one was meaner. "You gonna look a whole lot worse you don't let us have that wallet." He pushed a gun into Bo's side. It was nothing new. In five hundred decoys, Bo had been beaten, stabbed, slashed, and cut. A lot of guns had been stuck into his face and ribs. Not that he got used to it. Especially when it was large scale, like a .45-caliber pistol, the gun that, so they said, fires a bullet that goes in like a nickel and comes out like a basketball. That kind of firepower breeds a certain amount of respect. Bo was thinking, I hope this guy with the gun isn't nervous, magicked up.

Bo was a soldier. The crime had to go down. Move too quick and all you get is hurt. You had to have balls and brains to work decoy in Harlem, and even then you could catch hell.

The young guy finished pissing on Tommy. He

shook his joint a few times, zipped up, and started back to meet his friends. Tommy could move now. He unlimbered his 9-millimeter and started sighting at the guy walking away.

The pair with Bo were hard at work. One took the wallet and the other kept the gun in his ribs. The one with the gun said, "Here's a little something gonna help you sleep." He hit Bo in the gut with the gun. Bo staggered, but he didn't go down.

I could see Tommy climbing out of the mattress. He had his gun out and he was wiping something off his jacket. I put my thumb and my finger to my forehead—a signal that these guys had guns. And I went in after my cock. That's where I kept my own gun. In my shorts. Some degenerate shitheel going for a wallet won't find the gun in your shorts. Even if he's looking for a weapon, a guy won't grab your balls that quick. Unless he's inclined in that direction.

These guys see Tommy chugging down the street after them. I didn't know if he saw my signal. I wanted to run after the guy with the .45, but my legs weren't working. I was slapping at them, trying to get the blood going. But they wouldn't budge. So I yelled out to Tommy, "Be careful. They got a gun!"

The three guys were moving out. They had a block lead on old Tommy. They were young and poor Tommy's forty and he can't chase like he used to. Meanwhile, I feel the circulation starting to come back in my legs, but they still weren't working right. I'm yelling like a maniac. "Be careful. They got a gun!"

A cab started coming down Third Avenue and I pull my badge and waved in front of the driver and ordered him to stop. The cab slowed down and I jumped on the hood. I had my legs up at the window. I'm still yelling at Tommy, "Be careful. They got a gun!" I turned and look at the driver. He's all fired up. He's got a cop on his hood and he's chasing bad guys.

These guys turn a corner and start down another street and the cabdriver puts it to the floor. He really took off and I'm holding on for dear life. As the cab passed Tommy, I yell, "Don't worry, I got the mother-fuckers!"

The cab pulled even with the three escaping men and Bo yelled to the driver, "Okay, stop!" The excited driver hit the brakes and Bo left the hood of the cab like a torpedo. He didn't even try to break the fall. He just relaxed, accepted it. He landed in the street, real blood mixing with the fake Number Three theatrical blood.

The three robbers split up and Tommy took off after the two closest to him. He finally stopped them, ran them down. Last he'd seen Bo, he was flying off the hood and he didn't know if his partner was alive or dead. He smiled and said in that strange John Wayne voice, "Well, Pilgrim, if you wanna make your move, now's your chance."

The two bandits looked at each other, then turned quietly and put their hands up against the wall.

The third bandit, the one with the gun, had turned and was running back up the street, past the spot where Bo lay in a heap. He didn't see Bo. Bo waited until he was on him, then jumped up. "Hey, asshole!" he cried. The man turned and had the gun pointed directly at Bo's belly. Bo had his gun out, too, but this called for something else. He leaned back and hit the bandit with a roundhouse to the jaw. The bad guy went down, dropping his gun. Then Bo fell. He was a mess, too. The bad guy got up and tried to kick Bo. But Bo was too quick. He grabbed his leg and threw him over. He hit him again, but he was too weak to finish the job. He picked up the loose gun, then lay down next to his prisoner and bled for a while, trying to catch his breath. The bandit was bleeding from his head and his mouth. Finally, he opened his eyes.

They loaded the three into the van and headed back to the Two Five. One of the bandits arrested by Tommy called through the mesh, "Hey, my man, you that dude they call Cowboy. Yeah, I know you. But who's your girlfriend?"

"That's my partner, Bo."

"Shit, man, it ain't fair, dressing up like that and shit."

"It's legal," replied Tommy.

"Yeah, well, it may be legal, but it's what you call unsportsmanlike."

They stopped by Roosevelt Hospital on the way downtown. Bo was worried about one of his prisoners. Thought maybe he broke his jaw, but all he did was rattle loose a few teeth. The doctor in the emergency room was more concerned about Bo. He bandaged his bruised rib and then got ready to go to work on the severe laceration on his face. Bo just peeled off the theatrical cut and handed it to the doctor. "It really ain't that bad, Doc," he said.

Tommy was in a bodega *picking up a couple of six-packs when the ten-thirteen came over the air. I was sitting shotgun in the van and the three prisoners we'd taken down were handcuffed to the seats. I was trying to explain to the one guy that I was sorry I had to put out his fucking lights, but he had to understand, you can't go around with a gun like that taking people down. I told him, "Hey, you'll be okay, you're lucky. A clean shot and I'd've cracked your jaw. What the fuck, man, you broke my rib."*

"Wish I'd cracked your fucking head," the guy says.

"Here I am, trying to talk to you like you're human and you still think we're on the street. You fucked up. I caught you. You'd feel a lot better if you just let it go at that."

"I'll feel a lot better tomorrow, son-of-a-bitch. I'm back out, I'm watching for you."

"I'm done trying to talk to you. You're an asshole."

I look at the other two. "Why do you hang around with this asshole?"

Meanwhile this call comes in. Ten-thirteen. Some guy's shooting at cops up at 118th Street.

Tommy shakes his head, pulls a couple of cans of beer off the six-pack, hands one to me. "Your ribs okay?" he asks me.

I nodded.

Then he turns to the three guys in the back.

"Any of you assholes want a beer?"

Then we rolled.

Chapter 18

They left the van sprawled outside of the social club on 118th Street where the siege was taking place. They would have to leave the prisoners alone in the back; they didn't have a choice. Tommy put his finger under the nose of each man. "You guys sit tight," he said like a parent who knows that the children are capable of inconceivable mischief. "No funny stuff." He moved his index finger down the line. "All right?"

The gunman was last. He gave Tommy a bad-ass sneer. "Don't try it," said Tommy with a weary shake of his head.

One of the prisoners cleared his throat. "Man, are we in some danger out here?"

"You don't like taking chances?"

"I do not like getting my ass shot off on state time."

"Are you asking if you are in the line of fire?"

They all nodded.

"Let me put it this way: If I were you guys, I

163

wouldn't call undue attention to myself," said Tommy.

"Man, you hafta be outa your mind," said the youngest one, the one who was sweating. "We are prisoners. I don't want to stay out here. I want to go to fucking jail."

"The man has a point," said Bo. "This is very rude of us."

"Hard times call for hard measures, partner," replied Tommy.

"I tell you what, this is not right," said one of the bandits. "This is a definite violation of my rights."

"He's got a legitimate beef," said Bo. "Tell you what. If you happen to get killed in the cross fire, I will personally see to it that your complaint is processed."

"Nothing could be more fair," said Tommy. "Listen, fellas, we have to run. Have a couple of beers, relax. This won't take long."

He and Bo leaped out of the van and ran across the street, toward the action. There were two cops on the scene already. One was wounded in the leg. They were still waiting for an ambulance. The wounded cop's partner was kneeling, talking to him, trying to comfort him. Then he noticed the reinforcements.

"What've we got?" asked Tommy.

"We got a freaked-out cokie. He killed one guy in the bar. For nothing. Shot the poor fuck in the head."

"Where's the cokie now?"

"He's upstairs. Heavily armed. Got my partner as we were coming in."

Bo leaned down to check out the wounded cop, who flinched, seeing this human wreck with fresh blood all over his face coming at him. Then the wounded cop recognized his fellow officer. "Dietl, what the fuck happened to you?"

Bo shrugged. "I was out on decoy."

"Looks like you lost."

"Listen, why don't we go back in there and get that guy," said Tommy. He was still holding his can of beer. He handed it to the wounded cop and took out his 9-millimeter.

Bo recognized that voice. He was working with John Wayne again.

I had to climb up onto the roof of a car to grab the fire escape. I could feel my side, where I had hurt a rib. But the blood was pumping. I shimmied up the fire escape and got to the third floor where the guy was holding out. I couldn't see the guy in the room. The window was too dirty to see through.

I was a little winded and I stopped to catch my breath. It would take Tommy and the uniform cop a few minutes to come up the stairs. I got my jacket off and wrapped it around my arm. Then I heard it. Tommy was pounding on the door. I heard him call out, "Police!" That's when I made my move. I smashed the window with the arm covered with the jacket and jumped into the room. And there was this guy. Huge. I mean, the room was too small for him. I took a quick look around and saw a dead guy on the bed. And then this fucking gorilla starts coming at me.

I could hear Tommy pounding on the door, trying to get in, and I figured that I might need help with this one. So I edged around and managed to open the door. The gorilla, meanwhile, is going for the window. So I tackle him. He kicked me hard in the gut and we both come up facing each other. He's got his gun and it's pointing at my crotch. I got my gun out, too, but this looks to me like a standoff.

Meanwhile, Tommy is screaming, "Don't move, you son-of-a-bitch!"

I am calmly saying, "Put the gun down, man. Please don't make me shoot you."

This gorilla is screaming at me in Spanish and his hand is shaking like a motherfucker and all I can think of is where this thing is pointing. The uniform cop is yelling, "Shoot the fucker, kill the son-of-a-bitch!"

I am pleading for my balls. "Please, man, please. Don't make me do this." My fucking eyes are wet and I am inching closer and closer to the gorilla.

"Come on," yells the uniform guy. "Blow his ass away. He hit my partner."

I wanted to blow that fucking uniform asshole away.

Meanwhile, the gorilla isn't moving. I'm coming closer, my voice is soft and pleading and I pull the old trick. I look past him, like there's someone on the fire escape, and I yell, "No, don't!"

The guy flinched. Had to. It's the oldest trick that there is, but there is no man alive who will not flinch. He looked away for a second. Not even. But that's all it takes. I hit him in the face. Then I kicked him. Knocked the gun out of his hand.

But this gorilla wasn't finished. He still wanted to fight. He's coming at me, like a fucking hulk. And he's looking at my gun. He wants to grab my fucking gun.

The uniform cop is yelling, "Will you for Christ's sake kill the bastard? What's the matter with you guys?"

"Bo doesn't like to do that," said Tommy in his cowboy way.

The gorilla kept coming. He was pushing against my arm, trying to reach my other arm, the one with the gun. So I really bore down. I pulled on his arm, then yanked it up with everything that I had. I could feel it coming out of the socket. And I could hear it snap. The guy screamed.

Tommy put the cuffs on him.

"He's all yours," I tell the uniform guy, who looks a little puzzled. "Look," I explain, "we were on our way downtown when we got your call. We've got some prisoners in the van. I'll help you with the paperwork tomorrow."

"You got prisoners in the van?" he asks. "I can't believe you guys."

The gorilla is looking at the body on the bed. The one he killed. "I don't even know this fuck," he says.

The ambulance was waiting when they got back to the van. The street was crowded with cops. In the back of the van, the prisoners had finished both six-packs. There were some girls leaning in, talking some shit with the prisoners. "Come on inside," the prisoners were saying. "Have a little fun."

"You guys take care of business?" one of the younger prisoners asked. The mood had lightened since they were left in the bull's-eye.

"Couldn't you save us one fucking beer?" said Tommy. "Pigs."

"We not in any hurry," said one of the mellow prisoners. "We could stop, get us some more six-packs."

"You buying?" asked Bo.

"Man, if I could be buying, I wouldn't be sitting back here in this deep shit."

One of the other young ones had a suggestion. "We could drive around for a while. Help you make some arrests."

John Wayne answered. "That'll be the day, Pilgrim."

"That's bad, the way you do that shit."

"Did you hear that? That was that Clint Eastwood, am I right?"

"You're walking a mighty thin line there, mister. Nobody makes light of the Duke."

"Shiiit, I knew that was the Duke."

"Duke? Duke who?"

"Duke. You know. Chuck Norris, fool."

"Bad. Real bad. Oh, man, I never thought I'd be laughing on my way to jail."

"Hey, who's hungry?" asked Tommy, and they stopped for sandwiches and beer.

"No point sending them to jail hungry," said Tommy. "They feed them rat shit in jail."

Almost light, and Bo was feeling grungy. They'd turned over their prisoners to the court officers in the Arraignment Part of the Criminal Court. Nothing to do now but wait for the prints to come back from Albany. It would be hours. Bo asked Tommy to cover for him while he went home and got cleaned up, maybe see the kids.

"Fine," said Tommy. "I'll be over at Maruffi's getting a few pops."

By the time Bo got back, Tommy had that glazed look. He was sitting at a table, drinking with a couple of other anti-crime detectives. The more he drank, the more interesting the stories.

". . . And then the guy turns around and pisses on my box spring."

The other cops let go a couple of belly laughs, turned to their drinks, and took deep swallows.

"I took it very personal," said Tommy.

"You loved it," said one of the detectives. "You straight-looking guys are always into that weird shit."

The other one picked up the beat. "That reminds me, they got that report in on Duke Wayne."

"Watch it, now," said Tommy.

"No shit," the detective said. "It's the truth. Hey, you don't believe me, ask your partner."

Bo had just come back from home. The decoy makeup was gone. He was scrubbed and combed and wearing a three-piece suit. It was hard to tell that this clean-cut man—someone who looked like he might be a hot young tax attorney—was rolling around the gutters of Harlem last night, fighting muggers and killers. If you looked closely, you couldn't miss the fact that the suit was a little tight in the arms and shoulders. Not attorney flab. A lot of muscle.

"I can't believe this guy," said Tommy to the other two detectives. "I've been out with him all night, he gets cut up, beat up, and fucked up, then he washes that shit off his face and I don't even know him when he walks through the door."

"You are one crazy maniac, working a decoy up there," said the first detective to Bo. "You have got to be a first-grade nut."

"Me and Tommy just do it to make the rest of you assholes look like shit," said Bo.

"I'll tell you what's even more off," said the second detective. "What no one can picture is why you didn't shoot that fuck in the social club. This guy has murdered two people, right? Blown them away. He's already shot a cop so we know he's not afraid of a citation. Now he's trying to get your fucking gun. And you talk shit to this scumbag. This is what confuses the rest of us and makes us nervous."

"It's the legend of Bo," said the first detective. "The

man has twelve hundred arrests and he's only fired his weapon once. And even then, he wasn't aiming at anyone. This is not normal."

"I get along without the gun," said Bo.

The first detective shook his head. "If I'm in some fucking alley and a guy's coming at me with a gun or a knife, I'm gonna put him to bed."

"Definitely," said the second detective.

"Okay, let me ask you, what would you do, Bo, say you're in that situation? You're in some fucking alley with your gun out and a guy's coming at you with a knife in his hand and you can see in his eyes that he wants to open you up. Would you ace him?"

Bo thought about it. "I'd let him get real close," he said. "I'd be trying to talk him out of it, telling him, 'Please, man, I don't want to have to shoot you. Put the knife away. Let's talk about it.'"

Bo got up, moved away from the table, acting out his scene, because that's the way he did things—vividly and with a sense of theatrics. "I'd watch him carefully. Very close. I'm the only one who knows I'm not going to put a hole in him. He gets right up on me. Fakes to the left, like we're one-on-one in basketball. I know he's coming in, my gun's dead on him, but I still can't do it. Got to clock him."

They didn't need to see the scars on his hands from the knives he was a little slow in stopping. Everyone knew that Bo would sooner bleed a little than kill someone.

"One less thing I got to carry around in my head," he explained. He looked at Tommy. "Fingerprints back yet, partner?"

"It's only three hours, partner. But don't worry. I know the guy who hit you has a sheet a mile long."

They sat drinking for a while. "That arrest wasn't any good, you know," said the first detective.

"What are you talking about?" asked Bo.

"Well, Cowboy told us the story. You exposed your prisoners to danger. They'll be out on the street tomorrow. No fucking shit."

"The fucking guy put a hole in my ribs," said an indignant Bo.

The first detective shook his head. "Doesn't matter. Look, the whole system's corrupt. What I say is, mind your own fucking business, don't take any money if you don't have to—and if you do you're on your own. What are we gonna do? We're surrounded by assholes."

"You could have saved yourself a lot of trouble," said the second detective.

"How's that?" asked Bo.

"You should have shot the guy."

"You know," said Tommy softly to the second detective, "you've got a kind of violent attitude."

Easing into his John Wayne voice, Tommy said, "Let's ease on up to this bar, Pilgrim, see if this town has any who-hit-John."

"That reminds me," the first detective said to Bo. "We were just telling Cowboy about that report that came in on John Wayne."

"You mean the one about how he really died?" said Bo. "Heart attack in the men's room with the little boy in the stall with him and all that shit? That what you mean?"

"They don't know if that's what killed him," the first detective said. "It could have been the heroin."

"You assholes! If any of you had seen *The Quiet Man* you'd show a little more respect."

"You know why they called him 'The Quiet Man,' don't you?" asked the first detective. "'Cause it's hard to talk with a dick in your mouth."

"Pilgrim, you're starting to get me mad."

It took all day to retrieve those fingerprint files. Fucking computers are down or somebody has a coffee break—who knows? We're sitting in Maruffi's and putting them away and I'm playing my game. Got these big Tactical Patrol Force cops coming in and as soon as they see me, they start lining up. Somebody wants to put me down. So off comes my coat and my vest, down goes my tie, and we start arm wrestling. Big motherfucking TPF cops who think they own the fucking city, and here's this little guy beating them. Did my heart good to put a little humility in those arrogant fucks.

Finally, late in the afternoon, the prints come back from Albany. I look and I see that this guy who tried to mug me, the one with the gun, had already done time for murder. Two years. This killed me. Two years! For a fucking murder.

Not only that, I know that the anti-crime guy is right. He's gonna walk on this because of one bullshit legal trick or another. I see this and I say, "Ah, shit, let's head back to Maruffi's. I need another drink. He's gonna walk, isn't he?" I say to Tommy.

He shrugs. "He's guilty, isn't he? Then he walks. That's how they keep us employed."

"I got an idea," I tell him.

He wants to know.

"No. Never mind. Just trust me. Maybe we got a shot at a little justice."

"What are you talking about?" he wants to know.

"We're gonna put this asshole on trial."

Chapter 19

The Arraignment Parts are located on the first floor of Manhattan's Criminal Courts Building. Each of the courtrooms is a huge bay, buzzing with the chatter and the urgent whispers of criminal overload. Lawyers are busy telling clients the exact longitudinal location of criminal liability, relatives emit a steady whine of special pleading, and cops sit back, displaying by their unbuttoned, floppy arrogance scorn for the entire procedure. Court officers, meanwhile, bang again and again on the old wooden railings, demanding a show of respect that simply doesn't exist. The railings are dented with generations of indifference. Still, the braying of the court officers serves as a reminder of original intent, that in these chambers, one is supposed to encounter, if not perfect justice, at least an impartial referee.

Meanwhile, in front of the long wooden fence inside the courtroom that separates the spectators from the participants, the bloody line of alleged felons moves through the room in sullen slow motion. The accused muggers sit next to the accused killers until their names are called and then, suddenly, as if in an instant, the judge is asking if the accused is aware of the charges, if he has a lawyer. The prosecutor prods, demanding bail—usually more than the wretched prisoner can raise—and then the prisoner is ushered away, behind the clank of steel, back into the bowels of sullen slow motion.

It is a scene of endless chaos and woe.

The idea came to Bo when Tommy said that he couldn't recognize him after cleaning off his decoy disguise. If Tommy couldn't recognize him, then maybe others would have the same problem.

So, Bo called some friends who work behind the bench—clerks, court officers, correction officers—and everyone thought that it was such a great idea that there was no shortage of volunteers. Even a stenographer said that she would work late.

AR-2 was supposed to close down for the night at five o'clock, leaving AR-1 to handle night court. But not this night. Tonight, AR-2 would be in session.

It was just after seven at night when the two detectives brought their prisoner, the mugger with the gun, into AR-2. "All rise," announced the court officer. "Court is now in session, the Honorable Richard Beauregard presiding."

The stenographer had a tough time not laughing out loud when Bo entered the courtroom wearing the judge's robes.

But the prisoner didn't catch on. He didn't notice the crowd of detectives in the back, plucking cans from six-packs of beer, clapping each other on the back, wallowing in the fact that one of their own now sat in judgment—even if it was only a joke.

"Bring forth the prisoner," said Judge Bo, rapping the gavel.

The prosecutor, a plainclothesman, handed the judge the criminal record of the prisoner, which Bo read.

"Hmmmmm," he said, then looked up from the paper at the prisoner, shook his head, and went back to reading.

Another plainclothesman, pretending to be the court-appointing defense attorney, whispered to his client, "This looks bad."

"Whatchew talking 'bout?" replied the client. "Nothing happened yet."

"No, no," said the lawyer-cop. "I know that judge. He's a hanging judge. This looks very bad. Did you hear the way he hummed?"

Bo put the paper down and looked down upon his prisoner. "Your name is Frank Murphy, is that correct?"

"That's right," he said, still not worried, still unaware that anything unusual was taking place.

"I have your record here, Mr. Murphy."

The stenographer pretended to be coughing. Judge Bo shot her a look of judicial restraint.

"Read back that last remark," ordered Judge Bo.

"I have your record here, Mr. Murphy," replied the stenographer.

"Good. Very good." Then he turned to the prisoner. "But not that record, Mr. Murphy. Not good at all."

There were giggles in the rear of the courtroom. Judge Bo rapped his gavel. "I will clear this courtroom if I have to."

"Sorry, Your Honor," said one of the detectives,

staggering to his feet, holding a can of beer up in salute.

"Where was I? Oh, yes. Your record. You were arrested in 1973. Four times. In 1975, five times. In 1977, you did two years for murder."

"Yes, that's about right," said the accused, looking down at his feet.

"You think that's funny?" said an aroused Judge Bo. "You are amused by this . . . what's the word?"

"Appalling," offered the defense lawyer.

"Yes. Thank you. This appalling display of bad behavior? You think that is something you can just ignore?"

"I din't say nothin'," said the prisoner.

"Well, let me tell you something, Mr. Murphy, you are what we call a bad guy," said the judge.

The prisoner kept staring down.

"A very bad guy."

"I object," said the defense attorney.

"On what grounds?"

"Well, I'm not exactly sure."

"Well, you are a bad lawyer."

The court officers were standing at the door, making certain that no stranger wandered in by accident.

"You know why you are a bad guy?" asked the judge.

The prisoner stood there, not moving, not comprehending. This was unfamiliar courtroom behavior, but then judges could be very strange. He knew that from cellmates.

"You do all this, you have this extensive record, and just last night you rob a police officer."

"I did not know he was no cop," said Murphy in

his own defense. "The man did not look like no cop."

He was looking straight at Judge Bo. He did not recognize him. Bo bit back a smile.

"You are a menace to the community," said Judge Bo. "A menace to New York City. I intend to make an example out of you. I am therefore sentencing you to life in prison. You will be taken from this place to a high-security prison where you will serve for the rest of your natural life at hard labor."

The words were like a bell and the prisoner's legs buckled.

"Judge, oh, my God!" He threw his hands up to his face and began to wail. "You can't be doin' this to me, Your Honor. You can't be doin' this to me!"

"Take him away," said Bo.

The two detectives grabbed him under the arms and began walking him back to the pens.

"Please, Your Honor," said the prisoner, still crying, still trying to appeal to the bench.

"What? You want to talk to me again? I don't want to talk to you."

"Please, God, don't do this to me."

"All right," said Judge Bo. "Bring him back."

The detectives brought him back before the bench. It took Murphy a while to recover. He was sobbing, but then it gradually subsided. "I don't know why you doin' to me like this, Your Honor. Don't be doin' this to me."

"Weellll," said Judge Bo. "I don't know. I have not heard one word of apology."

"I am sorry. You just don't know how sorry I am."

"Do you, Frank Murphy, hereby apologize for all the crimes you have committed and swear by

Almighty God that you will never commit another one again?"

"I do."

"Do what?"

"I apologize and I swear."

"You tell me an Our Father right now. Say a prayer."

Frank Murphy got down on his knees in the courtroom and made a short, clumsy prayer, swearing that he was heartily sorry for offending and for committing crimes and pledging that he would never ever do another bad thing in his entire life.

"Word of honor?" asked Judge Bo.

"On my mother's grave," replied Murphy.

"All right," said Bo. "I'll knock it down to fifteen."

"That's still a lot of time," said the fake defense lawyer.

"Make it fifteen days," replied Bo.

Then they led the bewildered Murphy back to the holding pens.

"This court is adjourned to Maruffi's," said Judge Bo.

We were standing there at the bar afterward and it was funny. We kept picturing this guy Murphy, when they bring him before the real judge the next day. He was gonna be very upset. The man would not know what the fuck had hit him. He thinks he's got a two-week ride and he's gonna get hit with two years.

After a while, we got quiet and we just drank. It was a very sobering thing, that courtroom. To sit up there, on the bench. To have power. To put on those robes and know that it meant something. That feeling that there was someone on the bench who knew what it was like on the street. Not some asshole judge who had been a lawyer and a political hack and had his head stuck up his ass. But some street cop who knew what it was to put it on the line every night.

Maybe it didn't mean diddly squat, but it felt good. It felt, just for a little bit, like justice.

Chapter 20

There were things about Bo Dietl that whispered trouble. But they were only rumors. The chiefs had heard about the gambling and the free spending. The attitude of the superchiefs toward that way of life was always a blue-nosed reproach.

"You live well, don't you?"
"I work hard. I need to relax, Chief."
"How do you manage?"
"I worked a lot of overtime."

One year I broke the record in overtime. A letter came down from the police commissioner saying we couldn't have this kind of overtime. I was single-handedly breaking the municipal budget.

So this Inspector, Grunwald, a good guy, wrote back a letter saying that he went over every single one of my arrests. There were more than a hundred for the year.

Every one of them was a felony. Every one of them was checked and double-checked and they were all quality arrests. If you don't want him to make overtime, give him the day off, Grunwald wrote. He went right up against the PC. This officer works extra hard. Overtime comes with it.

It's nice when they back you up.

When Chief Howard was in charge of Special Operations Division, he calls me down. This is in 1977. His walls were filled with maps and diagrams of the Waldorf-Astoria. The shah of Iran's wife was coming into town and this was a time when there were demonstrations and security was important. But the protection of the wife of the shah was not why he called me down. Howard brings me into his big office and he's got all this shit on the wall about sectors and precincts and diagrams and he says, "You know, I have a very big responsibility here, but I can't think of anything but Bo Dietl."

I do not say anything.

"I got the shah's wife coming into town, and am I thinking of tactical problems? I am not. I am thinking of Bo Dietl. Bo Dietl this, Bo Dietl that. I heard about you with the Legal Aid."

I shifted my weight. There was a little trouble with this Legal Aid lawyer who I did not get along with. He used to always try to nail me for brutality when I brought in the crazy decoy arrests. His name was Lee James. Short hair. Defender of the Black Panthers. So, one night in court, he gives me one of these stiff-shoulder things. Hits my shoulder when he walks past. So I clip his shoulder when I walk past. He goes running to the judge and charges that "Bo Dietl assaulted me, Your Honor."

I said, "Wait a second, Your Honor. Hold it right there. If I clopped this little punk here, I would knock him into tomorrowland. I would like it put in the record, Are there any marks on this man?" And the judge said, "No marks." I said, "This man has a serious problem. His liberalization of his brain has taken effect into his cerebellum." This is exactly what I said.

The judge was not amused. He sent a letter to the department, which went into my folder, but it was no big deal. He said there were allegations, but that they were unfounded.

Chief Howard is saying that he is sick of hearing about Bo Dietl. He's even dreaming about me at night. Me and the complaints. Me and the overtime.

I was actually taken off the roster and put on the telephone to cut down the overtime. I was making too many collars. In one month, I made 180 hours overtime. I'm supposed to be taking home six hundred dollars every two weeks and I'm more than tripling it. I'm taking home two thousand. They stick me on the telephone and they make me a driver for the captain. So we're on our way to some meeting and I drop him off and I see some guy snatch a purse. Bang, I got another collar.

The captain comes out from his meeting and he sees me handcuffing the suspect and he blows his top. "You're not safe!" he screams.

But it's not for the money. Money does not mean shit to me.

Well, this is not strictly true. I enjoy having money in my pocket. I always did. It comes from my childhood when money was so tight. I remember how lost I felt when my parents would be arguing about money. I couldn't wait to go out and earn my own. I have earned a living since I was nine years old. I took my brother Alan's paper route. Then, later, I lied about my age and got a job in the diner where my father was the cook. We were dishwashers, Alan and me. God, the things we did to that pickle barrel. I will never eat a pickle from a diner.

So I suppose money has some meaning. It gave me independence. I needed that. Especially in my house.

My father's problem with the gambling saw to that.

I did not go for horses, but I liked to play poker. I never let the poker thing get out of control, but it was pretty bad. The poker games we had in the back room of that bar on 119th Street were wild. A lot of money changed hands. I remember betting a thousand dollars on the turn of a card. Wild games. Guys would walk out owing $20,000. All the money you had on you, you'd lose. If I had a big overtime paycheck—$2,200—it was not unusual to lose it all and end up owing another $2,000.

It was sick.

Now I had this friend, Millie. She was married to this Wall Street vice president—a millionaire, really rich. And she liked me. I met her at Forlini's in about '75. She took me to all the fancy places—21 Club, the Russian Tea Room. Introduced me to good food. There was nothing between us except friendship. We'd go out, her and her husband and me, and go dancing. She was thirty-six and liked to be seen with a young cop. The husband didn't mind. He turned out to be one of my best friends.

One night, I did very well in the back room. I had a couple of thousand bucks extra, which always burns a hole in my pocket. I hadda find someplace to spend it.

Now, where else are you gonna spend some extra money?

Hey! Let's drive to Atlantic City! These two cops, one sergeant and plainclothes Buddy Dentato, from Anti-crime decide to come along. I borrow Millie's Cadillac and she phones out ahead and gets me a $25,000 line of credit.

There were three new hotels that opened that year—this is 1978—and we book a room at the Bally's Park Place. Actually Millie booked the room. This was no ordinary room. It was right next to Vikki Carr's room. It had a hot tub in the center, fireplaces, the works. Complimentary liquor. Complimentary bowl of fruit. Flowers. We were like kings.

The sergeant—call him Logan—owned a carpet company on the side, so he was doing pretty good financially. Until he went on this trip with us.

He had about $10,000 between him and the other cop, but he also had a credit line.

We started gambling. It was insane. At one point, I saw Logan bet $7,000 on craps. On a don't-pass line. Seven fucking thousand dollars. He didn't make it, needless to say.

Logan ends up losing more than $30,000, in addition to his fucking carpet company. The whole schmeer.

It was a Friday night and I can't believe that we all lost all this fucking money. I had an American Express card and I took all the advances I could get on it. I lost a total of $15,000. This is a fucking disaster.

We were all very depressed.

I said, "Oh, fuck it." We line up martinis, straight up. We had a martini race, Logan and I. We had twelve each lined up. And we start racing, drinking them down, one after another. I knew it was insanity. He was *drinking them down, he was very honorable, but I was cheating, spilling a little out. I would drink one, spill the other out. I was not consuming as much as he was consuming.*

But we are both fucking bombed.

We gotta get up to our rooms, right?

There was a female security guard standing by the elevator. She was well and truly built. Logan is bonkers, going, "C'mon to my hot tub, baby, we're going to have a party!" I didn't know it at the time, but he grabs her by the tits and pulls her into the elevator. I got my own troubles maneuvering through the opening. We fight our way up to our floor and the door opens and we spill out into the corridor.

Logan is crooning, "C'mon, baby, we'll have a party in the hot tub," and he's pulling her.

The security guard is on her radio calling for help while Logan tries to drag her off the elevator. But she breaks loose. We stagger into the room and Logan falls down on the floor. And I can see this little puddle spreading around his groin.

"Sergeant Logan, you are a disgrace to the New York City Police Department," I say.

All of a sudden, there's this pounding on the door. All the help shows up. About thirty members of the security force. They want to lock us all up.

I say, "Hey, calm down. Take it easy. Sergeant Logan here is a member of New York's finest. A superior officer, in fact. Sergeant Logan, show these people your badge." Of course, Logan is gone. He can't show them his eyes. The man is barely capable of breathing. So I have to reach down and pull out his badge. I show it to them. I show them my badge.

"This does not excuse his grabbing a guard by the

tits," says this very officious asshole who is in charge of security.

"Certainly not," I agree. "I could not agree more. Grabbing tits is certainly an offense, if he really grabbed someone's tits. It could have been inadvertent. But let me ask you something. Does that man look like he could grab anything?"

And I point down to this smelly wreck of a human being who is pissing all over the hotel carpet.

"Maybe he brushed against your chest, ma'am," I say, but she is still furious. "I will apologize to you for him because this man is not capable of speech, as you can plainly see. If he did anything wrong, I am sorry, and I am certain he will be sorry tomorrow morning."

"Okay," says the officious head of security. "We won't lock you up. But you have to leave the hotel."

"You mean, get out of town by sundown?"

I call Millie and tell her that we have disgraced ourselves in Atlantic City. We have been kicked out of the hotel room. "No problem," she says. "Just go over to the Playboy Hotel and Casino and I'll establish some credit there."

So we moved over to the hotel, but Logan was destroyed. He couldn't take the depression. We left town the next day.

Logan has since become a born-again Christian.

"What about this feud with Roy Innis?"

"I wouldn't call it a feud, sir."

"What would you call it?"

"A professional relationship."

In December, me and Tommy were working anti-crime and we get a call, men with guns at CORE *headquarters. This is over at 130th Street and Park Avenue.*

They wouldn't let us in, and since this is a very touchy area, we do not push it. Finally, after about fifteen minutes, they open up. I go running up the stairs and I see this big desk and there's this big guy behind it. I didn't know who Roy Innis was, I didn't know that he was the head of the Congress of Racial Equality. All I know is that we got a call about men with guns.

So here is this man and he is sitting behind this desk and next to the desk is a chair and on the chair is a briefcase. He sees me coming up the stairs and he points to the briefcase, and one of his flunkies grabs it. The flunky is just a kid and he starts to run with the briefcase and he starts to throw it behind another desk. I grab the case and there's an automatic in it. It was clearly Innis's bag—it has his passport pictures, stuff from Libya, stuff marked top secret, a lot of his crap.

"Roy," I say, "I think this is your bag."

He says it's not his bag.

"Okay," I say, "then the kid is under arrest for the gun, and the rest of this crap is going to the United States attorney."

The kid goes to trial and Roy Innis does nothing. The kid hangs for the gun.

This is no racist thing. I am not coming after Roy Innis because he's black. I know something about what makes for a stand-up guy. You don't let some poor seventeen-year-old kid take the heat for you. I know that much.

But I am not through with Roy Innis.

About five months later, sometime in the late summer, we get another call, same location. "Holding one, grand larceny."

I go shooting up the stairs and it is very dark. One light bulb, and in the hall, there's a guy laying on the floor. He's fucking bleeding all over the place. His eyes were closed and it looks to me like he's unconscious.

All of a sudden, there's Roy Innis. And he goes, "Oh, no! Not you, Bo!"

So I say, "What's going on here, Roy?"

"We got ourselves a common criminal."

"Really?"

"We did justice with this common criminal."

"This guy looks like he's dead. What did you do to him?"

"We tracked him down."

"What did he do?"

"He was stealing my car radio."

I turned to Tommy and told him to call an ambulance. I also told him to call the sergeant because I figured that we are going to have a situation.

"A common criminal," says Roy.

"The man is bleeding from every part of his body. He is very seriously hurt. If the cops did that, you would be the first to march down to the DA's office and prosecute."

He's glaring at me. There are about fifteen guys and they're all glaring at me. Finally, the ambulance comes and this "common criminal" still has not regained consciousness. I ride over to Harlem Hospital with him. The man has broken ribs, a punctured eyeball, contusions everywhere. He's in very bad shape.

"What did they do to you?"

He looks a little worried. "It's okay," I tell him. "You don't have to worry. What did they do?"

"They tortured me. They beat me for an hour and a half."

"Who? Who did that?"

"Roy Innis."

"How do you know it was Roy Innis?"

"I know him from the neighborhood. He's the one beat me with the lead pipe. They held me down and they kept asking me, Was I from the NAACP? Was I from here or there? They put a knife to my throat. They pissed on me."

"Are you sure it was Roy Innis?"

"Positive."

Then they took this guy away to the operating room. I go back to the precinct and I tell the sergeant that I am going to lock up Roy Innis for felonious assault.

"Oh, no, no," he says. "You have to call the district attorney."

I call one of the midnight DAs and I get the same wet-pants treatment. "Oh, no, I gotta call my bureau chief. Oh, not Roy Innis!"

Finally, the Manhattan bureau chief gets on the phone and he says the same thing. "Bo, you cannot lock him up."

"Bullshit," I say. "I got a complaining witness. I got all sorts of evidence that he committed felonious assault. If a cop did this, the district attorney's office would be down here this second locking his ass up."

My captain calls me in and orders me not to arrest Roy Innis. "Go down to the DA's office in the morning."

We had a great meeting the next morning. Everyone is scared shitless that there's gonna be riots in the fucking streets if we arrest Roy Innis. Nobody wants to move on this. All sorts of red faces. "You'll never find witnesses," says the DA. "No one will testify against the head of CORE."

"Bullshit," I say. "My partner and I will find witnesses." And we did. For two days, we went out and we found five witnesses. Middle-aged people, reputable people. They saw ten or fifteen guys grab this poor slob, run over him with the car, beat him with a lead pipe, and drag him back to the CORE office.

They'll all testify. They saw Roy Innis there, holding up the radio and saying, "This shows the people of Harlem that anyone fucks with CORE, this is what is going to happen to you." He makes his little speech on 129th Street and my witnesses all heard it.

So I end up locking up Roy Innis. He shows up with a mob of lawyers.

The guy who stole the radio turns out to be a bullshit little thief. Never convicted of anything but petty larceny. A Vietnam veteran. Pathetic.

But they beat us at the trial. It was the guy's record for petty crime.

Afterward, everyone said, See, that's what happens. But I hate that thing about people being afraid. I hate bullies.

"You like the holding pens, Officer Dietl?"

"I don't know what you mean, sir."

"Well, there are reports that you have yourself placed inside the holding pens so that you can administer summary judgment."

"I don't know what you are referring to, Chief."

"You're another Frank Serpico, aren't you?"

"I have over seventy-five medals and awards that you have given me. I have been mugged five hundred times. That's documented. That's right in the files that you gentlemen have in front of you."

"You like to fight, don't you?"

"I do my job."

There are several cases. Several. In the Two Five, I came off of one decoy and they got two perps in the holding pen. These guys are cop killers. They're supposed to be taking these guys down to be booked and they can't get them out of the cell.

"Why not?" I asked one of the detectives.

He shrugs. "They don't want to go."

"They don't want to go? What are you talking about? We're the cops. Fellas, nobody else is coming."

You know, I always knew that about the job. From the go. When I went into my first dark alley and I didn't really want to go, but I knew—nobody else is coming. I'm a cop. I have to go down there. "Put me in the pen," I tell the detectives. "Nobody else is coming."

I made the cop killers come out.

"We know about your Arab friends."

"Nothing wrong there, Chief. I checked with the ethics panel."

"They give you gifts?"

"They give me gifts. Nothing wrong there, either."

"And your friend Felix who owns Adam's Apple. He gives you gifts? I suppose he never gave you a bottle of liquor?"

"A bottle? He has given me a case. He's my son's godfather. Frankly, sir, I do not believe that it is anybody's business if it does not interfere with my job, if I do not use my official capacity."

The chiefs sat there.

And Bo got angry: "You know, I have to say this. I have been sitting here for a couple of hours with my bad back and I am in tremendous pain. I do not go out sick. I work every day with this pain. Because I love this job. You gentlemen have the power to give me that detective shield and you have the power to take it away. You guys are playing with my life now. This is all I have to say."

"Thank you, Officer Dietl. Please step outside for a moment."

It wasn't long. They called him back.

"We've reached a decision," said Chief Murphy. "If you stay out of trouble for six months, you will be promoted to detective."

Bo was momentarily taken aback. Then he spoke. "With all due respect, I thank you for your time. Thank you very much. But it's not stopping here. You cannot do this to me. I'm going down to see the mayor, because I work for him, too."

Bo left, bent over with pain. He was fighting the tears, but he wouldn't cry, not in front of them.

Chief Guido, the most antagonistic, was furious. "I'll put handcuffs on you before you leave the job," he called after Bo.

Bo headed back to the Two Five. Everybody knew what had happened. There was an air of gloom in the squad. Bo picked up the phone and dialed the office of Chief Guido. "I am going down in a blaze of glory," he told Sergeant Stevens, standing next to him. "Pick up the extension. I want you to hear what I think of Chief Guido."

The phone rang.

"Is Chief Guido there?"

Meanwhile, Sergeant Stevens was trying to signal Bo. There was another call.

"Chief Guido here."

"Uh, hello, Chief, this is Officer Dietl. Did you call me?"

"No."

"Uh, I got an important call from Chief Murphy. Can I get back to you, Chief?"

"You call me back," said Guido.

Bo went into the next room where Chief Murphy was on the phone.

"This is Chief Murphy."

"Yes, sir."

"You know that guy you called a scumbag?"

Oh, Lord, thought Dietl. That's it. A week ago, in the midst of his frustration, he had called Police Commissioner McGuire a scumbag. It had gotten back to McGuire.

"That guy whom you called a scumbag, you know what he said? He said, 'I don't know where I'm gonna be six months from now. Bo Dietl gets promoted tomorrow.'"

When he called Chief Guido back, Bo put on an act. "How ya doin', Chiefy? You little softy. I know you voted for my gold shield. You're not fooling me. If you were here now, I'd give you a big kiss."

The last thing Bo heard, before he hung up, was Chief Guido yelling into the phone:

"Dietl, I will put fucking handcuffs on you before you leave this job!"

Chapter 21

It wasn't a clean reward. The promotion came through as promised. On the following Monday, Bo Dietl reported to the auditorium of One Police Plaza and, in the presence of his family and friends, was handed his gold shield. There were television interviews and there were handshakes, and, underneath, the bad feelings remained. The chiefs were not done with spite.

It didn't take long to see it. Bo had been promoted to detective through the Bribery Review Board, and it was the custom after such a deserving promotion to grant a choice of assignments. When he returned to the Two Five, after the celebrations and ceremonies, there was a message waiting for Bo.

"Dietl to the Seven Five."

Word filtered back from Chief of Detectives Sullivan that there would be no transfer, that the assignment to the Seventy-fifth Precinct in Brooklyn was final and permanent. "Bo Dietl will die in Brooklyn," was how Chief Sullivan put it.

The Seven Five was located in yet another Brooklyn ghetto—East New York. It bordered on Queens, and was, in fact, only a few miles from Bo's home. Which was not one of its charms for Bo. He preferred to keep his professional and personal lives separate.

East New York was a high-crime area, having led the city in homicides for a couple of years. The average was about sixty homicides annually compared to the citywide average of fifteen per precinct. But the body count isn't what made it bad. What made it bad was a kind of low-energy sour gloom Bo found among the members of the detective squad.

When he first reported in to the Precinct Detective Unit, he stopped off in the coffee room. One of the precinct detectives came over. It wasn't a friendly greeting.

"So, you're that anti-crime guy," he said with a trace of malice. "You're the hotshot with the big reputation."

Bo ignored the provocation and went about the business of making coffee.

"We heard about you," continued the precinct detective. "You're the guy who sat on all that information in the nun case. You didn't give it to the Detective Bureau."

So here was the abiding resentment. Here was the grudge, out in the open. Here was the petty jealousy, right in his face.

Bo's first reaction was anger. Here was a colleague turning on him in ignorance. But then he sat down at a table and went through the entire case with the precinct detective. Every detail. He told the detective exactly what he had done in the nun case.

"You can believe what you want to believe," he told the detective. "But what I have just told you is the truth. No bullshit."

There was a lieutenant in charge of the Seven Five's detective unit who knew the true story of the nun case. Herbie Hohmann passed the word around that Bo Dietl had earned his gold shield—he had broken the nun case.

But this didn't alter Bo's first bad impression of the Seven Five.

First day, a gun case comes in. A civilian walks in off the street and makes a complaint that a neighbor pulled a gun on him.

In the Two Five, you hear some guy has a gun, you roll. The idea is to get the gun off the street. The guys in the Seven Five didn't work that way. They got on the phones. They're calling him up on the phone to ask him nicely to come in with his fucking gun.

I went out. I went to the address and I grabbed the guy and I bring him in.

When I bring him in, everybody is looking at the gun like it's a big deal. Like they never made a gun collar before. They look at me like I got two fucking heads. "Hey, what's with you guys? Aren't we fucking cops? What are we, Boy Scouts?"

The trouble with these guys here is that they were demons for statistics. Close the case. Close the case. That's all you heard: Close the case.

It didn't matter if the case was actually solved. It didn't matter if there were two guys involved in a shooting. If you got one, that was enough. It didn't matter if the other guy was the shooter. Got one, mark it closed.

This actually happened. We had a shooting by three hoods. Three gunmen, one corpse. So the detective catching the case manages by some miracle to capture one of the gunmen. They mark the case closed.

I went to the lieutenant. I said, "Hey, Herbie, there are two more perps out there. We only got one and I don't even know if he's the worst one. He may not even be a shooter."

He tells me to get back to work on another case. This one's closed.

This is a homicide. So we got two killers running loose.

They were great for putting out wanted posters. You got a good mark if you put out a wanted poster.

Most of these guys just wanted to do the paperwork and go home. They didn't socialize. They didn't go out drinking after work. They didn't want to go out for a meal. They just wanted to go home. They weren't all-out cops, like the guys in the Two Five. It was a real boring place.

Still, it was police work and he was a detective and Bo Dietl made the best of things.

One day, there was a murder in a subway station. When Bo got to the station, Herbie Hohmann was having a territorial dispute with a Transit Authority Police lieutenant. It reached a pushing-and-shoving stage. Hohmann motioned for Bo, saying he would "catch" the case.

Real babies, thought Bo.

Suddenly, a report came over the radio of a robbery at the Jehovah's Witnesses Kingdom Hall off Sutter Avenue.

"Bo, you take the robbery," said Lieutenant Hohmann. "Forget the homicide."

I walked over and there were, I believe, 180 victims. That's a lot of interviews. Three guys with ski masks and guns came in and stuck up the place in the middle of services.

Now, we had a lot of uniformed guys there, but I was in charge. And I take charge. "Let's get all the sixty-ones—the complaint reports—done."

Meanwhile a batch of anti-crime guys show up. My asshole buddies. They pitch in to help.

I split them up into groups. People who might be witnesses. People who saw or heard something. People who heard and saw nothing. I begin to get a description. One person said that they might even have recognized one of the bad guys when he lifted up his ski mask to get some fresh air. Another thought they recognized the voice. He might come from across the street, in the projects.

Someone else said they thought one guy had a silver tooth. This guy's ski mask did not go all the way down and the silver tooth stuck out. I start talking to the anti-crime guys, all of whom I know from my anti-crime years, and we begin to pop up with nicknames. Jaguar was one.

Now we are going through the night. It is me and the anti-crime guys.

The best lead was the guy with the tooth, and we find out, by asking here and there, that his mother belongs to the church. The nickname of the guy with the silver tooth is Jaguar. We find out the mother's name.

We got to the door of the apartment and the kid is not there. The mother comes home early in the morning and we explain to her that "There has been a robbery and we do not think that your son has anything to do with it, but we'd like to clear it up. We need your permission to search the apartment."

So, I write out a paper giving us permission for a consensual search. And she signs. We were there for about an hour, and we finally found the stuff in a linen closet. In a pillowcase. Rings. Bracelets. Watches. Cash.

This is not a case broken by genius. This is a case broken by hard work. By not being lazy. A lot of those detectives just poke around and go home. But I stayed there. Night and day.

Jaguar comes home a day later. All the time we are going door-to-door, searching, looking for clues. When he does show up, we're there and we grab him. Then we find out who his friends are and we grab them.

It was a very pure bust. All three convicted of the robbery.

It took me days to type up the fucking report. I am not accustomed to writing DD 5s—the detective reports. The lieutenant takes the report, reads it, crumples it, throws it in the garbage, and he says, "Detective Dietl, we are writing police reports, not crime thrillers."

Life in the detective command went on. Bo formed no partnerships, as he had done in every job he had had in the police department. One day he worked with one guy, the next day someone else. If he was lonely for the close relationship of a partner, he managed with what he could find.

One guy was a crybaby. Everything that happened, he went running to the lieutenant. Another guy was only interested in his Spanish girlfriends. And some of these guys did not have their gold shields. They were plainclothes working in the detective squad. And they were being picked on.

There was one big Dutch cop, about six-foot-four, really had it in for them. He saw to it that they caught all the shit details. I said, "Let's make a chart; we all take a shot at the shit details."

The Dutch detective says, "You stay the fuck out of this."

"Hey, we're all working together. We're all cops, whether we have a silver shield or a gold shield."

See, I remember what it was like to work as a detective with the silver shield.

The Dutch puts his finger in my face and says, "You are fucking with the wrong guy," and he swings.

That's when I clobbered him.

There was an inspector in the other room, as well as an assistant district attorney, and I am on top of the Dutch prick, punching the shit out of him.

Hohmann comes out and yells, "You two, into my office."

The guy is standing there, blood dripping all over him. The lieutenant asks, "What happened?"

"Nothing."

"Nothing?"

"We had a slight disagreement."

"Get out of here."

The Dutch cop had been a local tyrant in the Seven Five PDU. He had bullied the others into silence, enforced his own arbitrary control over assignments, and was unchallenged because of his size. Even the lieutenant stayed out of his way. After the fight, Bo Dietl was treated with respect. He was small, but if you looked close, you could see that the baby face had been pounded around and was beginning to look like a fist. The Dutch detective shook Bo's hand and stopped picking on the kids with the silver shields.

I started to get a bad feeling. The Seven Five was a depressing place to work. The people in the neighborhood were very poor. And there didn't seem to be much hope. I started getting depressed going to work every day.

Especially after the child-abuse case. I went on a robbery investigation to this apartment on a call and I saw these kids in another apartment. They'd been left there on their own. Two young kids, maybe three and four years old. Little girls. It was wintertime and there was no fucking heat. There was no electricity. All they had was a candle. There was no food in the refrigerator and roaches all over the place.

So I brought the two kids into the stationhouse. The lieutenant says to me, "What the fuck are you getting involved in this for?"

I said, "What are you talking about? These are kids. They're abandoned. How can I walk away from that?"

"All right," he says, "make out a sixty-one and close it out."

In other words, wash your hands of it.

But I can't. I start going to family court on it. I testified against the mother. She'd vanished. They had the kids taken away. Five days later, she shows up and they give the kids back to her. Where she was for five days, nobody knows.

"Leave it alone," says the lieutenant.

"Fuck you," I says. "I got kids and I'm not walking away." I go back to family court and I testify, trying to have the kids taken away from the mother. I said the mother is unfit and the kids would be better off in a foster home.

She's sitting there in the hallway outside of the courtroom crying and I blow up. "Now you're crying?" I yell. "You're crying for your kids now? Where were you for five days? Where were you when these kids were left with no food and no heat?"

The guys at the precinct were laughing at me, but those kids were better off. I saw to it that they didn't go back to that home.

The lieutenant chewed me out. "You're supposed to be a detective," he says.

"I'm sorry, Lieu, but first I'm supposed to be a human being," I say, but he doesn't understand. None of them understood.

There was another time when I was on a homicide investigation and I am canvassing the area and I ring a bell and a kid comes to the door. About five years old. Bare-assed naked. And filthy.

"Where is your mother?" I asked the kid.

He giggles and there were two other kids there. They were triplets. All naked. All filthy. I mean, shit all over them.

I walk into the house and there's the mother. She's a foster mother and she gets money for taking care of these kids.

I take her aside. "Listen, I do not see any food for the kids and I do not see any clothing for these kids. I will be back in one week and let me tell you something. If this place isn't clean, if these kids are not wearing clothes, if I do not see food, I am taking these kids away."

And I did. I came back in a week. And the place was clean and the kids were dressed and the refrigerator was full. I kept going back there, giving the kids money, making sure that she was taking care of them.

I'd be driving down the street and see some kid and

I'd stop and hand him money. One mother came running out of a store, screaming at me. She didn't know I was a cop. She thought I was trying to pick up the kid.

It began to get to me. All that effort, all those years, and it didn't seem to make any difference. I began to feel like I was carrying a great weight on my shoulders. I began to get very tired. I'd park somewhere and begin to cry. "Please, God, don't let anyone see me cry." I would cry and I would say, "I can't take it anymore, I want to get out of here."

Maybe Chief Sullivan was right. Maybe I would die in Brooklyn.

Chapter 22

He kept a supply of Ballantine Ale locked in the bottom drawer of his desk. From time to time he would fight off the depression with a cupful of beer. It was a frightening thing, that he found himself so afflicted that he drank on the job, but the depression was long and hard. He didn't get drunk, but he needed something to soften the gloom.

Bo had tried to get back to the Two Five in a man-for-man switch—the police department had a policy of exchanging consenting policemen between commands—but Chief Sullivan's vow blocked the trade. Five times he found someone willing to switch and five times his request had been rejected without explanation, beyond the one he knew deep down. In desperation, he even tried to get transferred into Manhattan, anywhere out of the seedy East New York precinct. But he was a prisoner of the chief of detectives' grudge.

Despair played its part in affecting Bo's mood. But there was also that other loss—the loneliness of not having a partner. He missed the comradeship of a loyal friend. Someone to share the danger and triumph with. There was no one to appreciate his exploits and he found himself after work making a long drive to Adam's Apple, where Felix would play the audience.

In the meantime, Bo did what he always did when he got into trouble: He threw himself into the work.

There was a major Colombian drug dealer and he was in some kind of partnership with the owner of a social club on Fulton Street and Pennsylvania Avenue. Now, the dealer suspected that the owner of the club was fucking his girlfriend.

One day, he walks into the crowded social club and he shoots the owner in the head. The blood starts spurting out of the victim's head like a fountain. The people start diving for cover. The shooter looks around and says, "Anybody else want some of this?"

The owner is dead, flat down on the floor. The shooter then announces that the drinks are on him. This is not optional. Everybody's got to drink.

The blood is still squirting and the people are forced to have their drinks over the corpse of the owner. This guy means business. They all know him and he is one bad dude.

But this guy's not finished. He goes upstairs, to the second floor, where the owner of the social club had a room. There's a girl sleeping in the bed. He doesn't even bother to look. He shoots her in the fucking head. He doesn't even see her face, he just kills her. After she's dead, he notices that it's not his girlfriend.

Cold-blooded fucker. Lays down and takes a nap. But he is gone by the time we get there.

Me and this detective sergeant, Billy Campbell, catch the case. We get to the scene and the people are afraid. They tell stories that this guy is not afraid of anything. He is a long-lost junkie sicko.

So we do some tracking and some talking and we get an address on the guy. We take four other cops and we go to pick him up. I said, "I'll take the back door; you guys hit the front."

So, I'm still in the basement with another detective, trying to make our way upstairs, when we hear some crashes. There is a real commotion upstairs.

Campbell and the others ran into these four Colombians and they went berserk. I go running up the stairs and I see this guy—the murder suspect—trying to grab the sergeant's gun. He had his hand on the grip. He was big, too. I jump in.

I say, "Let go of the fucking gun." He doesn't let go. So I grab the arm with the gun—he has the gun by now—and I twist it around. I twist pretty hard and I break his collarbone in half. I actually pull his arm right out of the collarbone.

This pretty much takes the fight out of him. The other three guys vanish. We get him in handcuffs and we lock him up. We had him for double murder.

The DA's people start to talk about excessive force. This guy put three cops in the hospital and they are nitpicking about violence. The sergeant, Billy Campbell, had to leave the job.

They begin to interview me. They say that I punched the guy in the nose. It's like I'm the fucking suspect.

"Did you punch the suspect in the nose?"

"You mean the guy trying to get the sergeant's gun

and kill us, like he killed two people? That guy? Maybe. It was a fight. I was trying to save my fucking life."

"Well, Detective, this man looks like he took a beating. In fact his face looks a little bit like pulp."

"Oh, really? Did you know that he was wanted in three other homicides? I mean, apart from the two innocent people he blew away in the fucking social club. Did you know that? Oh, I should have been more polite, I know, but you see, he had this gun, and he was trying to kill me. He had already put three cops out of action so I figured maybe I could skip the amenities."

They loved sarcasm.

There are times you find yourself in a kind of Twilight Zone. We had this killer and we brought him in on a homicide, suspecting he was possibly involved with four other homicides. A bad man. Well, someone comes to visit him. His girlfriend. And she happens to be a cop. A female police officer was actually dating this creep.

I thought, well, maybe she doesn't know about this guy. I should give her the benefit of the doubt. Protect her a little, because she could be in real trouble if they decide that she turned the other way.

"You know, this guy has a long rap sheet," I tell her. She gives me a fish stare.

"He's got wanteds on half a dozen homicides."

She still does not blink an eye.

So then I see her talking to this cocksucker and laughing, like he's a fucking hero. I looked at her. She's blowing kisses to him through the bars. After I told her that he was a fucking murderer.

There was a lieutenant there from IAD—Internal Affairs Division. I knew the guy. Lieutenant Rivera. I said, *"Lieutenant Rivera, someone should nail her to the fucking cross because she has no business being on the fucking job. I just told her that this guy killed five people and she is throwing kisses at the guy."*

Turns out that she knew all about him bringing guns into the house. She knew that the guy was deep in shit. She didn't give a shit. If the guy snapped his fingers and said, "Jump through a hoop," she'd jump through a hoop. Eventually, she got thrown off the force. Which is a plus for everyone.

After a while, Hohmann put me on investigating homicides. I was good at it. I love investigating a homicide. There's a great challenge there.

First thing you do, you seal off the area. No one in or out. Then you round everybody up. Everybody. Then you bring them into the stationhouse.

Makes a difference when they are in the police environment. They get a little more cooperative. Out on the street they can be brazen. But the precinct house is very sobering. You have to grab them right away because once they walk away, you're never going to see them again. Those first few minutes are crucial. After that, people fall apart. You grab everybody at the scene and you put them all in radio cars and you bring them back to the precinct. You put people in one room, people in another.

Then you start to talk to people. Start to get the story. One piece of the story in one room, one in another. You fit the pieces together.

A Spanish kid, about seventeen, got shot on Pitkin Avenue and Pine Street. Six times.

The story was that this kid was supposed to be selling pot in the area. We had a bunch of kids who lived right above where the kid got shot. I knew that they knew who did it. They weren't talking, but I knew that they had the answer.

So I separated them good and I worked on them and finally, one broke. After one, the others broke. I got a nice statement, complete with the name, or at least the nickname, of the murderer.

I start looking for this guy and I am coming up blank. I got one telephone number, but it's no good. I work straight through the night. He is nowhere. No one knows where he is. I work through a second night.

Lieutenant Hohmann says, "Why don't you go home?"

"I can't."

"Tomorrow we'll come back."

"Tomorrow is too late."

I can't explain it to him. I don't even understand it. There's a drive. A lot of guys don't have it. But when I'm hot, I have to keep going.

Finally, I find out that the guy lives in Queens. His nickname is Jamaican. I kept calling and they kept saying he wasn't there. I went out there to the address with a bunch of cops.

This is near Springfield Gardens in Jamaica. We have three carloads of guys and if he is not in that house I am going to look real bad because I swore that he was there. Everybody is looking at me.

Someone suggests that we send for hostage negotiators.

"Bullshit," I say.

There was a Chinese restaurant on Jamaica Avenue. I go in and use the phone. A woman answers. "Listen," I say, "I'll tell you what: Your house is surrounded. We got a tank in the back. We got bazooka teams up front. We are burning the fucking house to the ground unless he comes out. You and your kids are gonna die unless Jamaican comes out."

"Oh, no," she cries, "don't do it."

"If he comes out, he won't get hurt. Tell him to come out with his hands on his head."

Jamaican comes out with his hands nicely on his head. Okay, so I threatened the family a little and maybe that's not so nice, but these people don't play by the rules, either.

Now, after we get this guy locked up, we call in the witnesses and they all make a nice identification, a nice tape, and we got a clean case. Then I'm driving them home and we stop at a bodega and we put away a few six-packs.

"Hey, if you ever need anything, just call Bo," I tell them.

You get to like people when you deal with them.

A few days later, I get beeped. It was my day off. A Saturday. One of the witnesses. In a big panic. I meet him at the stationhouse and he's a nervous wreck.

"What happened?"

"He's out there."

"Killer?"

"He had a machine gun. He said he was going to kill me if I testify against Jamaican."

I go out and round up my witnesses. All three of them. They are in very bad shape. The guy put the machine gun with a banana clip in all their faces and threatened to slaughter them.

So I call the DA and I want my witnesses protected.

The guy on duty tells me it's Saturday, I'll have to wait until Monday.

I said, "Hold it. These people have to be protected. They could be dead by Monday."

"I can't help you until Monday."

"I'm coming down there," I say, and we get into the fucking car and we stop off and have a few beers. Then we get to the DA's office and they make a tape. They describe the machine gun. Perfect. Semiautomatic. Everything.

Then I spot a DA who I happen to know, this guy Joel Cohen. "Hey, Bo!"

"I got a problem."

After I explain, he agrees to provide expense money and have the witnesses protected. I take them out to a hotel on Staten Island. The people looked a little startled when I bring in these three black guys from Brooklyn—this is a pretty white area. But my witnesses loved it.

"Don't worry," I tell them. "I'll bring him in in twenty-four hours."

I go after Killer. He has half a dozen murders on his file. I am working through the night again. I got a double-barreled shotgun in the car because I am maybe going to have to go up against a semiautomatic machine gun. So, now it is four o'clock in the morning and I am still running. I have an arrest warrant, but I do not have a search warrant (no reasonable suspicion).

And I have the guy trapped in a two-family house. Or, I believe that I have him trapped. I got the word from a good source and my sixth sense tells me it's right.

But I can't prove it. If he's not in there, I could get in real trouble if I order an assault. I have Emergency Services units all over the place. There are no less than thirty guys with machine guns and shotguns and vests on. I have brought in a fucking army. They're all waiting for my signal to attack. But I hesitate.

The sergeant says to me, "Are you sure he's in there?"

"Oh, yeah, I saw him."

I didn't. But I had to act confident.

So another brainstorm. I dial the phone and some-body sleepy picks it up and I use a real dumb voice: "Killer?"

"Yeah, what do you want?"

"Killer, is that you?"

"Yeah, what the fuck do you want?"

I drop the phone and go running. I give the signal and everybody charges the house. They were on the second floor of this two-family house. There are kids and women screaming all over the place. But no Killer. They do a search and come up empty.

"He's not here," says the sergeant.

"He's here," I say. "I saw him in the window."

Inside, my heart is pounding like a bastard. I am saying to myself, Oh, shit, he's not here!

But then I heard a noise. It was coming from the ceiling. They had these tiles that push up and lead to a crawl space.

"Quiet!" I say. "Everybody quiet."

There is no sound, except . . . something. Maybe.

In a hall closet there was an entrance to the crawl space. All the Emergency Services guys are standing there with their guns aimed up at the tiles. We know that he has a machine gun so it is very hairy.

"Easy, Bo," says one of the Emergency Services guys. He had a machine gun too and wears a steel vest. He goes up the ladder first.

I take the shotgun and climb the ladder into the crawl space. I point the flashlight into the corner, and there, with the machine gun next to him, is Killer.

I have to make this guy know that he is up against a hopeless situation.

"We got a hundred cops here with a lot of guns," I tell him. "Drop the fucking gun or you are a dead man."

Meanwhile, everybody below was yelling and screaming so that he'd know that there were a lot of psycho cops on the scene.

He gives up. We pull him down and find two other loaded guns with him.

The cops went crazy. I said he was there and I found him.

In less than twenty-four hours.

Chapter 23

There came a time when Bo realized that his gambling days were over. He could control the poker, but he began to bet wildly and recklessly on football games. Suddenly, he found himself forty-five hundred dollars in debt. At the close of the 1978 football season, he made the classic gambler mistake: he bet double or nothing on the playoffs.

It was the Oakland Raiders–Cleveland Browns playoff game. I was at home watching. Cleveland was ten yards out and going for a winning touchdown. Then Lester Hayes caught an interception in the end zone. I died a thousand deaths. I felt my insides drop out completely. All of a sudden, I owed nine thousand dollars. That was the end of my gambling. Thank God for the Arabs.

The Arabs came like a bequest. One day, during that same troubled season, Bo received a phone call from an old friend. "If you can use some extra money,

I could use a good man," said Abate. John Abate was a former cop with a street crime unit. He had retired from the police department and was now running security for the Arabs.

Bo had never taken outside jobs before. Not since the construction work almost ten years earlier. The overtime took care of his financial needs, and besides, he had always been too wrapped up in his work to bother with distractions.

But in 1978 there was a crackdown on overtime and he had gambling debts, and he needed the money.

"What kind of work?"

"Bodyguard," said Abate. "We need about four guys. Some Arab princes are in town and need some protection. Hey, it'll be fun."

Bo had a lot of time off coming and so he agreed.

They met at the Park Lane Hotel on Central Park South, where the Arabs had taken over a complete floor. They had twenty rooms for eighteen people. There were six security guards.

"The pay is good," explained Abate over breakfast in the coffee shop. "Ten dollars an hour."

"It's okay."

"That's ten dollars an hour and it runs for twenty-four hours a day. No matter how long you work. At least two hundred forty dollars a day, every day."

"The pay is good."

"The job is easy," continued Abate. "These people are members of the royal family of Saudi Arabia. They come to New York to spend money, to shop, to do business, and they want to feel safe."

"What are they afraid of?" asked Bo.

"Mostly blacks. They're scared shit of blacks. They've seen too many TV shows and they think they're gonna be mugged."

"What else do I have to know?"

"Well, do not look at their women. Stand up when they enter a room. And don't be surprised at the way they treat money."

"What do you mean?"

"You'll see."

You think people are people and that's that. But the Saudi princes . . . ! First of all, I am just a guy from Queens and, in some ways, these are very sophisticated men of the world. And they are royalty. They are accustomed to being treated with a certain degree of respect.

The other thing was that they were rich. Rich beyond anything I ever imagined. Anything they wanted—a piece of jewelry, a building—they bought it.

They carried around these cases filled with money. Actually, they didn't carry them around. The first morning, Prince Mansour—that's Prince Mansour Bin Naser Bin Abdul-Aziz—comes out of the hotel room, ready for business. Very polite. Very nice. They all had great manners. He hands me this case. Crushed leather. Beautiful case. Doesn't say a word. Just hands me the case.

He has to do what he has to do and I am there as his bodyguard. I keep my mouth shut, because I don't know what's going on here yet. We go around and at one stop, he asks for the case and I hand it to him. He puts it on a desk and he opens it. Inside the case are stacks of hundred-dollar bills. And Piaget watches. A bunch of ten-thousand-dollar watches. Not the kind you pick up on Forty-second Street.

Bo studied the Arab princes with the eye of a shrewd detective. He noted what they liked and what

216

they didn't like. He wanted them to like him. He sensed an important opportunity. They didn't like men who were moist with greed. They didn't like security guards who haggled about fees. Coarse, greedymen were soon gone. The ones who were quiet and accepting benefited from the royal largesse.

He knew without being told to sit in the front of the limousine. They were friendly, but the caste system was firm and important to them.

Bo understood. He recognized the trait. It was not much different from the protocols demanded by the royalty of organized crime. They, too, enjoyed the many signs of respect. They, too, insisted on dignity, loyalty, and snap attention. And both the Saudis and the Mafia shared one other very basic attribute: they always suspected betrayal.

Bo spent the day with Mansour, taking him to appointments, watching out for his welfare. Mansour was a high official in the government as well as a member of the royal family. His two brothers were army generals. The business end, which Bo eventually came to see, was to buy equipment for the National Guard.

If Mansour understood the complex and treacherous world of arms merchants, he was naive in Manhattan. When the Arab prince wanted to stop at the outdoor markets along Fourteenth Street, Bo said simply, but forcefully: "I don't think it would be a good idea, Your Highness."

The prince understood that this was the professional voice, a security consideration, and he instructed the limousine driver to keep going.

In the evening, Mansour wanted to relax. "Book a table," he told Bo. He didn't say where. But Bo understood that it would have to be somewhere in which the prince and his entourage would feel comfortable. Bo also understood that this was a test of Bo's competence—and, more importantly, his judgment.

I called up Regine's and I said, "This is Bo. We want two of the best tables, and one extra nearby for security. And what's your name?"

When you asked for their name they knew that you would take care of them. They set aside the best tables and when you came in, you handed them a hundred-dollar bill.

The Saudis didn't like to handle cash. Whenever you went out, at the start of a day or an evening, they'd give you a few thousand dollars and you would take care of all the bills. They did not want crass commerce to intrude on their person. Now, you could either do it honorably and be smart, or you could be a pig. Some of these former Secret Service guys and ex-FBI guys got greedy. Instead of handing the maître d' a hundred-dollar bill, they'd hand him fifty and palm fifty.

The Saudis never said anything, you'd never even know that they were paying attention or anything. But all of a sudden, you'd never see that guy again. It was unspoken, but they knew. They were not fools.

I never cheated them. I never tried to pull a fast one. And they knew that.

They would sit at the best tables at Regine's and they would order the best champagne and the best caviar. They would not drink liquor or party in their own country—it was against Moslem law—but it was all right in the West.

I heard the story about Mansour's father, Prince Saud Bin Naser Abdul-Aziz. Nice old guy. I took him around once. He was the brother of the king. He was supposed to become king, when he had been governor of Riyadh, the capital. But he drank too much. There was a kind of revolt against him back in the fifties. He was known as the bad boy of the crew. He loved wild parties and he used to sneak liquor into Saudi Arabia. Well, the religious people got offended and they executed twenty or thirty people. They spared him because his brother liked him, but it was a big lesson to the royal princes. They had their parties outside of Saudi Arabia.

Not that they were very wild. They looked pretty tame by my standards. The way you could tell that they were having a good time is that they would smile. They would never get loud or rowdy. They weren't troublemakers or obnoxious. They would just sit there and smile. Gentlemen. If they spotted a pretty woman, they would say, "She's cute. Why don't you invite her to join us?" The expensive hookers all knew the score. These guys were not stingy.

Their women, of course, would never come along. They would stay home in the hotel room. Men and women stayed very much apart.

At the end of an evening, when Bo tried to return the unspent cash, the aide to the Saudi prince simply held up a hand. They didn't like to handle money. There would often be hundreds of dollars left over and it now belonged to Bo.

The crushed-leather cases were kept under their beds. They did not trust hotel safes.

You had to watch their asses all the time. They were very innocent. They would leave their briefcases

219

around, just forget them. You had to pick it up and carry it. It was your responsibility.

And it was a heavy responsibility. One time I was with another prince and he was taking a big double suitcase from London to Geneva. "Be careful with that, Bo, it's got twelve million dollars in it." He was putting it in a Swiss account.

This same guy once had a bag ripped off in Marbella. He left it under the bed and when he looked it was gone. When I heard about it, I said I'd get a polygraph and find out what happened. He said, no, forget it, it would embarrass people. There were four million dollars in that bag and they just wrote it off. They never reported it to the police, to the hotel, to an insurance company.

There was a suspect, and that security guard stopped working for them. If he took it, I don't suppose the prince minded.

At the end of a week-long stay, when they left New York, the prince said he was happy with my work. They would call me again when they came to New York. One of the aides handed me an envelope. They took very good care of me.

They called from time to time and Bo always managed to keep enough vacation and overtime in his record so that he could go when they called. The money was good, but he also enjoyed their company. Now he was sitting at the same table at dinner. He was sharing jokes, giving them inside tips about where to go and what to do.

There were jealousies and intrigues that surrounded the royal family, as in any rich court. Ambitious men made ardent bids for favor and position.

The Lebanese were ruthless. These were the mercenaries who controlled access to the princes. Big, tough men. Liars. They would say anything to keep their position. They would do anything to keep you away.

One of the princes had this Lebanese guy who kept track of his money. I knew that the guy was a thief. Maybe the prince even knew that he was a thief. But he spoke the language, you know. The Arabs felt comfortable around people who spoke their language. Not that they didn't speak English well. Or French. They were well educated. But it was more like the Lebanese were one of their own.

You see that kind of thing in the neighborhood. Some guy wants Italians around because he knows what the guy is all about. Still, this one guy was stealing the prince blind and one day the prince got tired and the Lebanese guy was gone. Not a word. Just one day, he wasn't there.

You didn't ask about where he went, either. Everybody knew.

Pretty soon there were other Lebanese guys hanging around. There were always Lebanese guys hanging around. They wore expensive suits and ordered good wine and traveled with gorgeous women. There was a very international flavor to them. Because of where they lived. That world was a crossroads. Very cosmopolitan. And dangerous. So there was that added factor—danger.

They didn't like me very much. I was competition. The worst kind. I wasn't corrupt. These guys made skimming look like an art. It's an old habit in that part of the world. Graft, corruption, theft.

I did not take a penny I did not earn. An old habit. The other thing that gave me an advantage was

221

the fact that the Arabs liked me. I was a natural high liver. I had the same gusto for life. They liked that.

One day they were sailing the Mediterranean in a yacht. The next they were lunching in Paris. Bo flew into Marbella and had drinks with Adnan Khashoggi. He drove across Europe in an endless profusion of Ferraris and Maseratis and Mercedes. He developed a taste for fine wine and the clockwork attention of superior hotelkeepers and attendants.

The Lebanese and short-sighted colleagues who stole fell away, and soon—by a process of subtle selection—Bo was the regular outsider among the Saudis.

One of the young nephews was this fat kid, Mansour Bin Naser Bin Abdul-Aziz, same name as the uncle. He was about nineteen, but he looked older because of the weight. Kid loved to eat. Just at the time that the nun case broke, in October of '81, he calls me. "Bo, I have to go to Houston for medical treatment. I'd like you to come along."

There are some awards and things to clear up, but Mansour had heard some nasty things about Houston and he was a little concerned about security. Okay, so I get another guy. So, we know Houston. We can bring our guns—Houston cops respect New York cops—and we put them in a bag and we fly down there.

Houston is a rough place and I even feel a little nervous without a gun. We go to shop for some jewelry and these three mutts start circling Mansour. You could spot that they were bandits. So I walk over and I pull my jacket over and show my gun and these guys take off. The Houston cops come over and tell the prince that he was lucky I was there because these three guys were a team going around sticking up everybody.

Now I am a Saudi national hero. Mansour calls everybody and tells them the story. Nobody can believe what a great, heroic character I am.

I love it.

We were still there in Houston and we had a good time. They had all the medical tests and everything was fine and he says, "Let's go on vacation."

"Okay," I say, loving every minute of this kind of life.

"Where should we go, Bo?"

"Hawaii is nice."

"Make reservations."

So I make some calls, first-class this, first-class that. Blah, blah, blah. Meanwhile, we've still got our guns with us. So I call the Honolulu Police Department and I tell them we're coming and that we've got guns with us. They're supposed to get back to me, but we have to leave before we hear from them.

The private jet flies us across the country and over the Pacific to Hawaii. It is as lush and as lovely as all the travel posters. We leave a trail of money wherever we go.

Now, one of the Rolls-Royce drivers is being a real prick. He's trying to hit this guy for two thousand dollars a day. For doing nothing. So we say, "Listen, prick, don't be a fucking pig."

Well, the upshot was that he drops a dime on us. We're on a rented yacht and the cops come up and they say, "We got a report that you have guns on this boat." We admit to having the guns and we explain that we're

New York City cops and that we called first. They say, "Okay, we'll give you the guns when you leave Hawaii."

Meanwhile, they drop a letter to the New York City Police Department, which causes me some grief later when I went before the superchiefs.

Mansour, the younger guy, really likes me. I saved him in Houston. He really believes that I saved his life. We stop off in Disneyland and we have a limousine driving us around. We go to Knotts Berry Farm by helicopter. We hired our own bus to go to the San Diego Zoo. Anything and everything a person could want.

I had to stop off in New York to accept the award from the mayor for breaking the nun case. My face is on TV. My picture is in the newspapers. Mansour and all the other Arabs flip out. Look, look at this hero. Our hero!

He wants me to come back to Europe with him. "You've got to come. A reward for your great feat of heroism. Besides, I need you." He's still got some business there. On the plane, he shows everybody my picture in the newspaper. I'm a celebrity. Everybody knows about the nun case.

We go to Paris and we stay at the George Cinq.

Life was very, very sweet. We go shopping and Mansour buys a suit. "Give my friend a suit." Naser buys a leather jacket. "Give my friend here one." Thousands of dollars, just like that.

He's got these two Lebanese bodyguards. Monsters. One is former Special Air Service. The guy has to be 365 pounds. Mansour bets his mother ten thousand dollars that I can beat him in arm wrestling. And I do.

Mansour thought I was this fucking gorilla boy. We'd walk around Paris and I would lift up these little cars and put them on the sidewalk.

Meanwhile, he's teaching me about food and wine. We eat at the best restaurants. Stay at the best hotels. The man orders a four-thousand-dollar bottle of wine to wash down his dinner.

All the time he's whispering in my ear, "Bo, I want to make you a very rich man."

So I say, "Go ahead."

But that's the way with these people. They keep dangling those promises, but when it comes time to deliver, they have to go back to Riyadh or it's "I'll call you."

It's like a seduction. Keeps up this shit: "Bo, what do you plan to do when you leave the police department?"

He would send me first-class tickets to meet him in London. "Meet me for a meeting," was how he put it. And I would drop everything and go. He had a town house, a palace in Hampstead. We would sit down at this huge fucking table. Thirty feet long. There would be just him and me and his mother and enough food for two hundred, three hundred people. There would be whole lambs, veal cutlets, chickens, ducks, pheasants, turkeys. My brain could not comprehend it. Courses and courses and courses. We'd start at eleven o'clock at night and eat until three in the morning. This guy could eat. For four hours, we'd sit there and eat. I was the only one who could keep up with him.

I would take the Rolls-Royce and drive around town. He'd give me a few thousand pounds and say, "Go shopping, buy something."

I was like Prince Bo.

I stopped off one day at New Scotland Yard. I asked for their detective division and they take me to their MI5 or MI6—James Bond shit. They'd all heard about the nun case and I was a hero with these guys, too. One of their sergeants took a real liking to me and took me around. They had pictures on the walls of the IRA bombing of the bandshell. Men and horses all blown to shit. Very gross. This is what they were working on at the time.

In the basement, they had a bar right there and they took me downstairs and started to buy me pints.

The next thing, it is two o'clock and they close the bar down between two and five. I guess so everybody can sober up a little. They gave me medals and identification cards. It was a great afternoon. It was nice to see cops again.

By now the Arabs had stopped paying Bo as a bodyguard, as well as treating him like one. Now he was one of the entourage. He arranged to buy furs and jewelry, and wrote himself a 10 percent commission. They understood. It was business.

Mansour was persistent. What would it take to have Bo leave the police department and join his entourage? Bo wrote up a proposal: $500,000 up front. Then $200,000 a year retainer. Bo made it sky high on purpose. He wasn't ready to leave the police department yet.

They had me come to Riyadh, in Saudi Arabia. I had some trouble getting in. Problems with customs. And then I had to wait at a hotel while they were getting their business in order. So I was on my own for a few days. I realized that I hated this place.

I could not help thinking of Mansour's table. That thirty-foot table with enough food to feed a couple of hundred people.

That was hard for me to take. That was impossible for me to take.

Chapter 24

It was a daffy life; one day Bo was basking in the sun of Marbella, the next he was hunting down killers in back alleys of East New York. One night he dined in Maxim's in Paris, and the next he was eating Big Macs on a stakeout on Atlantic Avenue.

Whenever he came back from one of his off-duty jaunts, the men in the squad room at the Seven Five would say, "Where this time, Bo?"

And when he told them Morocco or the Bahamas, they didn't beam with pride, they didn't share the pleasures vicariously, they became sour with envy.

Still, the interludes with the Arabs did provide Bo with some respite from the drudgery. The cases he solved now were obscure and buried in statistical chaff. There was no glory in Brooklyn.

But there was gore.

It was raining very hard on that night. I remember the rain. I've never seen rain like that. It didn't stop.

I was off that night, but I told Gina that I was working. I was going out to meet friends. After I left the house, I called the office to tip them off, in case she called, to tell her I'm out in the field. I get Joe Hall on the phone. He was one of the white-shield detectives. He was practically alone, holding the fort. A lot of guys were off. It was April 15, 1984. Palm Sunday.

"Hey, Joe, I'm going on Plan B tonight." This is a code that means that you're supposed to be working but you're not.

"Bo, I think we got five dead," he says.

"What?"

"Maybe six. Maybe seven."

"Get the fuck out of here."

I'm standing in a leaking phone booth, no raincoat, near the toll plaza at the Midtown Tunnel. Maybe this guy is joking, but I don't hear that in his voice. I hear something else.

"What's the address?"

"Ten-eighty Liberty Avenue."

"I'll be right there."

So much for Plan B.

The first thing that I do is head for the precinct. It's always good to know what the tactical situation is. I get there and Joe is looking very shook up.

"We got nine dead," he says. "Bodies all over the place."

Just then the lieutenant comes walking in. They got him at home.

"What are you doin' here, Bo? Aren't you off tonight?"

"Yeah, well, I heard about this and I thought maybe you could use a hand."

"Okay. Come on. Let's run over there."

We get in his car and run over there and they won't let the lieutenant into the house. The chief of detectives was there and he ordered Hohmann to go back to the command. He had to coordinate the attack.

There were a lot of cops out on the street. Detectives, uniformed guys, commanders. Everyone looks very grim.

There's a guy on the door, although not many cops are going into this place. It's a house. Two-family wooden house. The crime scene is the bottom apartment. I have my shield out and I say to the cop on the door, "Seven Five squad."

And I go in.

You walk through the kitchen first. And there are a couple of cops in there, looking blank. Maybe a little frightened. They're slumped in the kitchen like there's something inside that they don't wanna see.

Usually, you go into a crime scene and there's a big racket. Cops meeting old friends. Saying hi. But nobody is saying a word here.

I go into the living room and it was the eeriest sight I've ever seen. The people were sitting up in chairs. Sitting up and looking out. With bullet holes in their heads. Bullet holes through their eyes.

One woman was sitting with a bowl of chocolate pudding in her hand. The spoon in her other hand. Like she's still in the act of eating the pudding. Only her head was back and there was a bullet hole through her mouth. A four-year-old boy was next to her. He had his arms outstretched, like he was trying to reach her. He had a bullet hole through the eye.

A television is playing. The people are sitting around, as if they're watching it. It looks as if they're watching. But the only thing alive in the room was the television set.

In the bedroom there's a boy on the bed, dead. There were two women in the bedroom. Dead.

I've seen a lot of murders, but I've never seen it like this. Not with people almost arranged. Almost peaceful. Some of them you had to look close to see the bullet hole. Just one bullet in the eye.

There were two women and eight kids dead in that apartment. The kids went from four to fourteen.

Whoever did this left a baby alive. A fifteen-month-old baby. They found the kid under the bed. It was hard to believe that it was an act of conscience that let that baby live.

A captain with twenty-five years on the job walked in and walked right out. He was sobbing. Emergency Services guys, who see everything, were standing in the kitchen, afraid to go any further. The forensic guys were standing away. Not going into the rooms. Like it shouldn't be touched. Like nothing should be touched. We shoulda just shoveled dirt on this house and buried it.

There was shock, but there was also calculation. Bo wanted to work on this case. He left the murder house and stepped out into the rain, which felt like air to breathe. He got a ride back to the precinct and cornered Herbie Hohmann in his office.

"I have nothing," he told the lieutenant. "All my cases are cleared up. All my files are up to date. I am free and clear."

"I'm giving the case to Jimmy McCalvin," said Hohmann. "But you're on it. You can work on it, too."

I get back in the car and race to the scene. I start interviewing witnesses. I go after the kids. There's a video parlor on the next block where kids hang out and I talk to them. Then there are a lot of neighborhood kids who are eyes on the street.

I ship all these kids into the stationhouse and I start interviewing them there.

They were very nervous, these kids. Not just because they were talking to cops. They were used to talking to cops. They were scared because something evil took place right there in their neighborhood.

These kids are about fifteen, sixteen years old. Teenagers. And I'm taking statements and talking to them and not a lot of anything is coming out. But I have a feeling that nothing could go on in that area without somebody seeing something. Maybe they do not even know that they've seen something important. Maybe they have to be guided or pushed.

I have the feeling that the answer lies with these kids, and in the end, I was right.

From the beginning, the police department operated on the assumption that there was more than one killer in what came to be known as the Palm Sunday Massacre. The theory was that one man couldn't do it. It was physically impossible. It would take one armed person to keep everyone still, to make everyone remain in place, while the killer went methodically from person to person and fired bullets into their brains. If there were only one perpetrator, so the theory went, the victims would have scattered and tried to escape after the first shot.

There was no evidence that anyone had tried to save himself. There was no evidence of a struggle. There was no evidence that anyone had moved or even been alarmed. No bodies had been put back in place. They all went to their deaths, it seemed, almost willingly.

One person could not do it. Only two or more killers could explain that.

The other thing was that the people had been killed with two different caliber weapons. True, one man could have used two guns, but it supported the multiple-culprit theory.

It looked like a Colombian hit. That's what the Colombians do when they get burned in a drug deal. They wipe out the whole family. As a lesson. To discourage others.

Meanwhile, we have no less than eighty detectives working full-time. The chief of detectives, Nicastro, is down there every day. A lot of heat. A lot of pressure. One of the reasons being that on the night this thing went down, the police commissioner, Ben Ward, was out of touch. He was off somewhere for two days. He comes back and the press is howling about where he's been—not that he could've done squat. They just like to have the commissioner there to interview for the news. So he applies pressure of his own to break the case.

The routine: Detectives went back and checked all the cars in the neighborhood. They interviewed and reinterviewed people who lived on the street.

The phone tips coming in were jamming the system. There were thirteen hundred phone calls on a special hot line. The police counted 150 people named by anonymous tips. Jealous wives turning in straying husbands. Old scores being settled indirectly. Each name had to be checked.

Bo and Jimmy McCalvin started working together. Technically, it was McCalvin's case, although there were a lot of high-ranking detectives maneuvering to outflank the precinct detectives.

There was one very credible phone call. This guy calls and he's very cute. He says he can't be too open because he might get hurt. We have an open line for him whenever he calls.

"My name is Green Eyes."

"Hi, Green Eyes, my name is Bo."

"I can tell you the whole story of the massacre."

"I'm all ears, Green Eyes."

"I need to be protected."

"Green Eyes, you help us on this case, and I can promise you that no one will ever lay a finger on you."

"This is very dangerous, Bo."

"I know that, Green Eyes. I was in that house."

"Okay, it was a contract killing and I drove the getaway car."

He calls five, six times. He's putting us through hoops. Go to Prospect Park, wait until the phone rings twice, then answer it. We do what he says, and it was a jerky thing, but the guy knew so much about the case. Or, he seemed to know.

He tells us that it's a guy named Dominican. He was giving us tips that all checked out. But it checked out with other tips, which came from him. He would call in a tip—not giving us his name—"This was done by a guy named Dominic or Dominican," someone would say. Then Green Eyes would call and say, "Dominican." It checks out.

He had us running all over Brooklyn. Finally, he was going to give up the guy. The guy's name is Pachek. Guy is a sailor, belongs to the Maritime Union. Eventually, we arrange to meet this Green Eyes in the park. We track him down and surround him and grab him.

Turns out he's full of shit. He didn't know a thing. When we asked him some detail about the crime, he was blank. He only knew what he read in the newspapers.

"Why did you do this?" I ask him.

"I'm doing this for my book," he says. "I had you guys going, huh?"

We all wanted him indicted, but the DA says no, too much trouble, too flimsy, too this, too that. So we let him go. As he's walking out of the precinct, he points at Herbie Hohmann with his finger and smiles. Herbie goes a little crazy. He grabs the guy by the neck and pushes him against the wall. "If I ever catch you again, I'll kill you."

The big task force lumbered on. There were two or three meetings a day with the chief of detectives, as the investigators shared information or plotted new avenues. There was a big blackboard with the major leads written in chalk.

One lead was the father of most of the dead children, Enrique Bermudez. He was not home and escaped the slaughter. Suspicion inevitably fell on him.

He would not talk to us. Not at first. And he was a little nuts. He had some kind of drug history, so we know he's not eliminated. We know he's a dealer.

But for reasons I am not altogether clear about, he did convince a lot of the detectives that he didn't do it.

Here's the thing about Bermudez: He was a male nymphomaniac. He had to fuck all the time. Some female reporter for one of the papers got to him and he took her into the house and she spent the night with him. Who knows what went on inside. She writes this story about how she spent the night inside the killer's house. And she did. We know it's true because we had him under twenty-four-hour protection.

Meanwhile, we're guarding him and he is demanding two and three broads a night. We have to bring him the broads. All his girlfriends. The guy had to have women around. Every night. I guess he liked to talk to women.

He started to cooperate, I mean, we were allowing these girlfriends in to see him. Then he got a lawyer and he starts to pull back. He's playing a game with the DA and manages to arrange some kind of immunity.

The guy never breaks down. Until the funeral. He kept it in. And then at the funeral, he fell apart. Now, Jimmy McCalvin had an accident on Long Island and was off the case. So they can't give a case like this to a junior detective like me—three years in the division. So they bring in Jerry Magliolo. He's second grade and first rate. Magliolo picks me to work with him.

After the first few weeks, the task force was cut down to forty. After another few weeks, the investigation was whittled down to fifteen. Bo was still on the case.

A call came in—a tip—that this guy Bermudez had a friend named Chris Thomas. They were partners in the drug trade. They were more than partners in business—there was wife swapping and girlfriend swapping and every other fucking kind of swapping going on.

This guy Thomas sounded right to me. I mean, we had hundreds of names, but from the records, he was a whacked-out junkie. Totally crazy.

Well, Thomas lives in the Bronx and me and Jimmy McCalvin—he's back by now—go up to his apartment and we act like we're investigating a burglary. Thomas has a rap sheet filled with burglary. We go up to his girlfriend's apartment in the West Bronx because his own house in the Bronx has been burned out (by him, we later learn). "Have you seen Chris around?" we ask the girlfriend. "We want to talk to him."

"Oh, no," she says. "I haven't seen him."

We get back to the car and I tell Jimmy, "He was there. I know he was there."

Then he comes running down the stairs and his eyes are everywhere. A madman. I'm ready to go for my gun, but we're supposed to still pretend that this is a burglary.

When I saw him I knew what happened in that house in East New York. Chris Thomas happened.

We put him under surveillance. He is not going anywhere. We find witnesses who saw him shooting up his house in the Bronx. It's building and building. This is a prime suspect.

The problem is that we do not have a link. Something to tie him to the murders. So we go to the burned-out house in the Bronx and poke around in the debris, looking for clues. Lieutenant Hohmann finds a shell casing and, as it turns out, it matches the shell casings found inside the slaughter house.

Now we find other witnesses. People are terrified of this guy. He's a one-man terrorist army. He's been involved in a shitload of homicides—prime suspect— but everyone's too scared to testify. He's never convicted.

We start to recanvass the witnesses on the street on the day of the massacre. And one of the kids I spoke to changes his story. He did see something. He heard shots and then he saw a guy leaving the building.

The kid's name was Michael and he was very frightened.

Meanwhile, Enrique Bermudez cuts a deal with the DA. He admits that he and Christopher Thomas did a drug deal two or three nights before the murders. Thomas broke into his house and wanted more drugs. Bermudez wouldn't give him any more because he owed him seven thousand dollars.

He claims that he wasn't sure it was Chris Thomas who wiped out his family—he says he had a lot of enemies.

Bermudez agrees to a plan. He'll call Thomas and arrange a meeting. Thomas will probably bring a gun. We'll be waiting to jump Thomas and grab him with the evidence.

Finally, the DA says, "Okay, take him." The trouble was that we couldn't find him. We lost Christopher Thomas.

This blows my own plan to kill Thomas. I was going to have the shotgun at the Bermudez rendezvous, and frankly, I was going to kill him. I would have waited for him to pull his gun and then I would have blown him away and never lost a night's sleep.

Thomas didn't stay lost. We find him in the Bronx House of Detention. He was arrested for raping and sodomizing his own mother. That's the kind of character we have here.

We take him out of the Bronx and we bring him to Brooklyn and we got the precinct sealed. Couple of hundred cops mobilized because somebody is gonna wanna lynch this filth.

We arrange a lineup and bring the kid, Michael, in to pick out Thomas. I'm standing there with the DA, the kid, Jimmy McCalvin. And the kid is really sick. He looks green. And he is not identifying Thomas. We got

238

six other look-alikes in there and the kid is not making a move.

The chiefs started to get nervous. The DA is ready to close shop. There's no case here.

"Hold it," I yell. "Just wait a second."

I run into the lineup room and I turn everyone sideways, because this is the way Michael saw him— profile. I run back and Michael is smiling.

"Number three," he says, and we got him.

I give the thumbs-up sign to Chief Nicastro, chief of detectives, and a lot of respiration returns to normal.

One of the chiefs, Howard, sees me and says miserably, "I should have known Bo Dietl was in on this."

Chapter 25

The arrest of Christopher Thomas was a significant demonstration of timely police muscle. Civilian morale, crushed by the wanton slaughter on Palm Sunday, was revived.

Those murders had deeply darkened the public mood. It was terrifying that an unknown evil that could exist among us could explode with such ease. The very serenity of the murder scene lent a symbolic dimension to the threat. We were all helpless. The police, it seemed, could not defend innocents in their own home. Where was anyone safe? Where would it end? Who would protect us? Where were the police? Thus the absence of the commissioner during the first crucial days took on added significance.

After the quick arrest, there was, as there always is under such circumstances, a surge of euphoria, a proud puff of the municipal chests as the detectives displayed the prisoner.

This time Bo was included in the choreographed picture. He stood beside Christopher Thomas when he was brought to Central Booking to be charged with ten counts of murder.

Fifteen detectives were selected for special promotion for cracking the Palm Sunday Massacre. Bo's name was second on the list.

All the guys were hugging and kissing each other. Not only did we take this animal off the streets, but we are all gonna get promoted. It was terrific.

Actually, there was a long history to my being frozen in rank. I was a third-grade detective and Lieutenant Hohmann had been pushing for a year to make me second. He thought I was a great cop and he kept citing my work. But the applications were always turned down without any explanation—beyond the obvious unspoken explanation that it was me.

But now! Now? How could they deny me second grade now?

Well, they could and they did. We waited and we waited and no promotions came down.

Finally, we get word from One Police Plaza—no promotions for this case. The police department does not believe that detectives should be rewarded for doing their jobs. Furthermore, no one should be promoted for work on a single case.

This is pure bullshit. After the Son of Sam case, forty-five people were promoted. Sergeants, lieutenants, they all made grade money. The first thing Nicastro told us when we went to work on this was that there would be grade money for everybody involved. Nobody would be left out, he swore. So much for promises.

Meanwhile, the men on the list are pretty disgusted.

They begin to blame me. If my name had not been on that list, the promotions would have come down.

I can't say that I blame them. The insides of me start coming out again. It ain't right.

It's cold. It's a cold fucking department.

We are still working on the case in the summer. Tying up loose ends. Gathering up evidence for the trial. We are finding new witnesses. Interviewing Thomas's girlfriend, who drove him to the scene on the afternoon of the murders. Tracking Bermudez again and again, because, to this day, I cannot see how one person could do this thing. No matter who he is. This thing is still a mystery, as far as I am concerned, so there is some impulse on my part to find the missing link.

One day I walk into the precinct and there's a young girl behind the desk—two, maybe three years on the job and she's a sergeant. She's chewing out a friend of mine, a guy who's got nineteen years on the job. And she's yelling, "What are you doing here? It's not your meal hour."

This guy's about forty years old and he has to take this shit. I go upstairs and I'm sitting at the desk and I toy with the idea of putting in my papers. Just walking away. More and more assholes are going to be taking over the department. More and more jerks who are only good at passing tests. No one gives a shit about Chris Thomas. It's like that old complaint—they got one guy, they can mark the case closed. Nobody else but me gives a shit.

And I cannot get over that little girl yelling at my friend.

No one's ever going to yell at me like that. I swear it.

But I do not want to do anything rash. So I take some time off.

It was a commercial flight to Paris. TWA. Bo and Mansour had the entire first-class section to themselves.

"You have solved this big case in Brooklyn," said Mansour.

"I had a hand in."

"Bo, Bo, why do you not come with me? Let me make you rich."

Bo had heard a similar tune in the past, but now Mansour laid out the deal.

"You know, Bo, we have many business transactions. All legal. All aboveboard."

Mansour's brothers—the ones who were in the Saudi Arabian military—were in the market to buy arms. They needed equipment for the National Guard. They needed police shock batons, shields, gas masks, helmets, rifles, sniper scopes. Even water-cannon tanks for disturbances in Mecca.

"We are allocating two hundred fifty million dollars," said Mansour.

"Why are you telling me?"

"Well, Bo, there are four countries who would be bidding on such a contract. France, England, Germany, and the United States. So far, we have people in France, England, and Germany putting together a proposal. We have no one in the United States."

"You mean, I could bid for the United States?"

"I do not see why not."

Bo did not stop in Paris. He went straight to Riyadh, where he picked up a list of thirty-six needed items up for bids.

I was running around like a maniac, picking up catalogs, speaking to arms dealers. I was turning *myself into an expert on crowd control and market value and inventory. I was learning about markups and profits and commission and becoming an entrepreneur. Before this, I was just a cop and money was an idea that belonged to somebody else. But on this one transaction, I stood to make close to $15 million if they allocate $250 million. I was thinking about Swiss bank accounts and safety from worry. I'd never have to scrape to make the mortgage again.*

So, I throw myself into this whole hog. I got a lot of help from the Saudi army. I am back and forth five times. Meanwhile, IAD is going crazy, trying to figure out what I'm up to. They even follow me out to the airport a couple of times. They think maybe I'm some terrorist assassin. But I inform the State Department of my every move. I advise the police department in writing that I am attempting to act as an agent in some business dealing with the Saudi Arabian National Guard.

They are freaked fucking out. Here is this third-grade detective—a guy who has always been a thorn in their side, no less—who is making moves on the international arms scene. It has them crazy. They are trying to destroy me and here I am flying back and forth to the Middle East, Europe, whatever. Like Prince Bo.

I would take the nine o'clock flight from Kennedy Airport. Pan American, Flight 24, New York to Riyadh. With an IAD guy watching. You'd leave at night, watch two movies, fly through the day. It was a twelve-hour flight, but what with the time differences, it would be dark again by the time you landed.

I hate landing in Saudi Arabia. I hate going there. There would always be some kind of trouble with customs. Always some kind of hassle. They treat you like shit. It was like my identity was gone. I was nobody. But, I loved it when I was on a plane coming back to New York. That was a beautiful feeling— coming back to America. I could never think of living anywhere else. Not the Middle East. Not Europe. Never.

Nevertheless, I have to follow through on this deal, this possibility. I am pretty impressed myself. I do not know how to fathom fifteen million dollars. I am running around for two fucking months on this. Riyadh and America. I catch up with Mansour and he's running back and forth to Frankfurt and Munich. We talk like equals. It is business. He had his private jet again. He took great delight in my fear of flying. Frankfurt, Geneva, Munich, Morocco. Storybook settings. Except for Morocco.

"Come," he says, "I have to visit my girlfriend."

The trouble was that his girlfriend lived in Morocco.

I truly hated Casablanca. It was so poor. So depressing. I'd be in my hotel room waiting for Mansour, nothing to do for a day or two, and I'd go out for a walk. You couldn't walk around there without having your heart break. All these starving children. I started giving away my money in the streets. I'd come back to the hotel to get some more money.

Then we'd fly to Lebanon and that was bad, too. There was filth and poverty and danger in Beirut. I was always lonely for America.

I liked it better when I was busy.

The arms dealers were all very helpful. They understood what was needed—the papers and permits. They told me who to go to next. Walked me through it like a baby. I was getting to know these CIA guys and they were getting to know me. It's a fucking fraternity.

You start to talk shit with these guys and they recognize the breed. We are all merchants, with a twist of military and law enforcement. We have a common ground and the small details—the terms of the art— come easily. "What about these Malacca rifles with a one-meter drop sight?" I was getting expert in the best sidearm—a 9-millimeter because the ammunition is universal.

I break my head to see what kind of proposal I can put together and I put together a beauty. I figure most of these guys in the other countries are gonna go for the standard markup. That's between 10 and 20 percent. Add on expenses. I decide that I will not be greedy. I will take 5 percent commission plus expenses. Fifteen million is plenty.

Meanwhile, I still have to work. A multimillion-dollar arms dealer still has to pull his eight-to-four in East New York. Because, so far, this deal is still one of these dreams. Maybe and maybe not. I'd fly back, do my police tours, work real hard, build up some time off, and then I would fly off again.

Gina doesn't mind. She's used to my life. It is quick and it is hectic, but I put enough money on the table. And she knows that I am a good man.

The business of being a cop was getting hard. They would stick me behind a typewriter or a switchboard— anything to keep me off the street. And then there were the grand juries. All these charges of brutality. They kept coming up because all my prisoners survived. If I had put some in the ground, they wouldn't be around to make a complaint.

The DA thought he had an airtight case on me. It was the Hector Lopez thing. This is a guy who murdered two people, shot a cop, and then tried to take me out, too. The guys at the Puzzle Palace really thought that they had me.

It was an old story. You go down there and two guys on the grand jury are snaring sandwiches, one old guy is taking a nap, and another guy is deep into the sports section of the Daily News.

I am on the stand and the assistant district attorney does not waste any time.

"Do you admit to injuring Mr. Lopez?"

I didn't want to give him a quick yes, maybe fall into a trap.

"Well, did you hit him?" yells the DA.

"Yeah, I hit him. I hit him until he stopped."

"Don't you think it was a little excessive, Detective?"

"I don't know. The man had just shot and killed two people. Strangers. He didn't even know the people he murdered. He also just shot a police officer. Didn't know him, either."

"And you hit him."

"He was trying to take my gun. I figured he had a lousy history of using guns against strangers and I did not know this guy personally, so, yes, I hit him to make him stop trying to take my gun."

"Did you absolutely have to break his nose and dislocate his arm and break his collarbone? Wasn't that excessive?"

"What would you have done, Mr. District Attorney?"

"That's not the issue here, Detective Dietl. The issue is excessive force."

The DA stalked away, like he made some dramatic point. The juror with the newspaper rumpled it, getting the page turned. I was very frustrated. "Hey, wait a minute," I yelled. He looks at me with a very conde-

scending smile. "Hold on just a second. I think we've got one thing wrong here. I'm the cop. He's the murderer."

The smile came off the DA's face. "Just answer the questions I put to you," he says. He could see that there were jurors listening. All of a sudden, he could lose this one.

I had to rub it in. "That's what I've been doing," I tell him.

The DA turns away. He's not even looking at me. He's playing with his papers. But I don't want to let it alone. I make a speech: "What do you people want? Yeah, I messed the guy up. I hit him. I hit him hard. But the man was a murderer and he was dangerous and he was trying to kill me. If I shot him dead, if I put a hole in his brain, you'd be pinning a medal on me instead of giving me a third degree. But I hit him. You know why I hit him? Because I didn't want to kill him."

There were tears in my eyes. The room was quiet. Even the men eating sandwiches had stopped chewing. The DA didn't even look at me. "You're dismissed, Detective Dietl."

I got down from the stand and I had to pass by the jurors. I grabbed the newspaper out of the guy's hands. Just grabbed it. Then I glared at him. Daring him to say something. Nobody moved. Nobody said anything. There was nothing to say.

But now, all alone out there in Brooklyn, I kept thinking of that asshole DA's warning. "We know you down here, Dietl."

What could I expect? What could possibly happen to me? I am going nowhere in the department. Only, as one chief said, to jail. He'll see me in handcuffs. They didn't understand my connections to the wise guys.

I took Tommy back there to Rao's and introduced him to some of the guys on the Police Intelligence List. We go in back and meet this guy in a three-thousand-dollar suit. He hugs me and I hug him. Tommy looks a little embarrassed because this is a known criminal and maybe it's not smart to hug a known criminal.

We eat veal and drink wine and leave and on our way out of there I try to explain to Tommy that I grew up with this guy. I helped him kick a dope habit. I sat in his living room and ate in his dining room and there are half of my genes that are Italian. I do not do anything bad. I don't take any money. But I don't volunteer to put any organized-crime people in jail. Tommy understands. He knows that I am straight and honest.

The people in the department, the paper pushers, all think that I have guilty knowledge. Some asshole will always give me that wink that says I know something or someone that can put a fix in.

I'm tired of telling them it's not true. I'm tired of the detective who comes over to my desk and says, like one moron actually did, that he's working in an undercover and could I put him together with a hitman.

I tell him, "Get the fuck away from my desk, I got work to do."

On a few weekends, I get a call from another one of the young princes, Fahad. He was Mansour's cousin. Also a prince. Prince Fahad Bin Turki Bin Abdul-Aziz. He's about twenty-five and he's in the military. Went through all our American Ranger and parachute and Special Forces training. A real physical fitness fanatic. He'd have all his people get down and do twenty-five push-ups. Right in the middle of anything. "Give me

249

twenty-five." And these overweight, out-of-shape flunkies would have to get down and puff and try to do twenty-five push-ups.

Fahad had been using another cop to do his local bodyguard work, but the cop got greedy and tried to steal something and Fahad comes to me. He knows that I have integrity. You can leave a case full of money in the room and I am never gonna steal a dime. This is my reputation with the Arabs. The other thing is that he admires my strength. We get along.

He calls me up one day and he says, "Listen, Bo, go down to the Bahamas. My uncle owns the Grand Hotel. We're coming down there, a few of the boys, for a holiday."

I go down and we have the whole top floor. I check out the rooms, I check out the layout. I make sure that they stock up on good champagne and caviar. I get cars and rent a yacht, just in case. Fahad arrives by private jet.

I meet them and they kiss me on the cheeks, like the French, and they are very happy with the arrangements. There are a lot of girls down there and I make certain no one is lonely. I ask the girls if they'd like to meet the prince and they all want to meet the prince. Girls from Canada, Australia. Nice girls, not hookers. I give them free rooms, whatever. We had about twenty rooms and we are only using seven, so I can be generous. To them it's an adventure. And these guys like having beautiful women around.

We had the yacht, we had cars, we had a ball. It was one long party. The reason Fahad had this party is that he had a break from training at the Ranger school at Fort Benning.

We went fishing, we went scuba diving. I forgot, for a

while, the lousy feeling I had back at the Seven Five Precinct.

The parties were still lavish by any standards, but Bo began to notice small things. The most important thing was that the deal for arms and equipment was not moving. No one spoke of it.

He made his proposal and it languished. He knew that he had done his homework and that the other proposals from the other countries were more expensive and not as good. But he also noticed that the price of crude had dropped on the international oil markets. And just as the barrel price went down, so too did the flow of Arab money.

The Saudis started to cut back. In small ways. They didn't give away gold watches with the same abandon. They didn't take over a whole restaurant for one night. They watched the money that went out.

And finally, the Saudi government decided that they could live without the brand-new equipment for the National Guard. The $250 million budget item was dropped.

Chapter 26

It was September of 1984 when Fahad graduated from Ranger school at Fort Benning, Georgia. Naturally, there would have to be a celebration.

We took the private jet to San Diego. He has a home out there. "Let's go," he says, and whoosh. We take off. There were cars waiting to pick us up at the airport. Mercedes. Ferraris. Maseratis.

The house is on a mountaintop in La Jolla. A twelve-million-dollar house, with waterfalls into pools, with whirlpools and hot tubs. There was a discotheque in the living room.

We were there for about a week. On the night of the eighteenth, there was a party. A lot of drinking. And in the morning, Fahad was up like a Ranger, ready to go. I felt like an old man.

"Come, Bo, we go skydiving."

He didn't know about my fear of heights. He didn't know that I'd never jumped out of a plane before.

I thought I should mention it, in case there was anything special I should know about what I was getting into. And he said, "Oh, well, you don't have to go."

But I can't look timid, not to these people. "I'm going, just tell me what to do." I am not going to be a faggot. I won't say, "Oooohh, I'm not going." I won't be a fungus.

So Fahad gives me a quick course in parachute jumping. Do not tense. Relax. Roll when you land.

No sweat, I was a gymnast. I know how to fall. I can do it.

Meanwhile my head feels like it's coming off.

It was a big-bellied plane with a huge door and loud props. Bo couldn't hear anything. He wondered how he got into this—given his aversion to heights. But it would be all right. Most things turned out okay for Bo.

They got into the private jets and flew to a skydiving field in Perris, about twenty minutes away.

It was one of those short-takeoff planes. I kept thinking, I'm not really going through with this. It won't come to that. They'll stop it at some point. Trouble with the engine. Fog. Something.

But then we are off the ground and I am watching the earth fall away through this open door. I am watching the clouds go from above to below.

Then I see Fahad standing in the door. He turns to me and smiles, then jumps.

Then it is my turn.

I don't even remember jumping. Just the feel of the wind. And the chute coming out through my legs. I know that it's not supposed to go through your legs and I have this click of fear.

253

But then the chute opens and I see it unfold and I feel safe. I can see the others across the sky and I am singing and screaming, but you can't hear a thing. The wind is thick.

But it was beautiful. It was late afternoon, getting close to dusk—some moment between the time when you could see and when it was dark.

The worst is over. I am having a great time, singing and yelling, drifting to earth. They can't hear me, but I'm happy. I am thinking about the party afterward. I will get my wings and there will be a party.

The silence is stunning. I kept yelling and it was like swallowing my own voice.

No one told me about ground rush. They left that part out in the briefing. All of a sudden, the ground is coming up at me like a fist.

One minute I'm floating. The next I'm landing like a broken match.

I didn't realize that you have to prepare to hit the ground. My ankle just folded under me. The left leg. Folded and broke the bone and the ligaments. I could hear the bones snapping in my leg—one after the other.

I look down and I see this blood. I know I'm hurt and I'm yelling for help, but I don't want to sound like a baby. Fahad comes running over and I think they were more scared than I was.

The other prince, Bin Abdul Aziz, bent down and there was real fear in his eyes. I could tell that these guys really cared about me. It wasn't just an act.

They began calling their crew over and debating about where to take me. Someone suggests the closest hospital, but Fahad says no. He turns to me.

"Could you take the flight back to San Diego?"

"Yeah, sure. No problem."

The ambulance arrived and they tied up the leg. They wrapped it up and put a splint on it to hold it in place.

They loaded me back into the prince's jet and keep feeding me a lot of booze. Someone asked me if I ever smoked a joint. Never had, but this is a good time to start. They take out this thing as big as a cigar and I begin to puff away. The pain was bad and I would have done anything. It helped, along with the booze, and pretty soon I am flying higher than the plane.

It takes about half an hour. A private ambulance was waiting when we landed at the San Diego airport. The prince had radioed ahead. They had the team doctor for the San Diego Chargers waiting for me.

They rush me to the hospital and skip a lot of admissions bullshit because the prince is there and exerting a lot of muscle. I am awake when they operate. They had to put pins all up and down the leg. The bone was pretty badly shattered. It was a mess.

I remember sitting up in bed afterward, all doped up, thinking, There goes my running days. Not gonna be able to chase muggers down dark alleys anymore. Not gonna be the kid I used to be. The doctor comes in and he says that I am always gonna have a kind of a limp. Nothing dramatic. But I'll know when it rains. There will be days when it hurts very bad. I am going to have to carry around a lot of iron in my leg.

I was thinking, I'm tired. I was very tired.

The first serious thoughts of leaving the police department came as he waited for the bones to knit in California. Bo had threatened to quit before. He'd

255

always played with the notion of retirement. But it was not serious, a kind of professional Russian roulette. He'd never meant it. It was too much fun being a cop.

I like the job. I like the power. I like the guys. I like sitting up all night in bars and telling war stories about the job. I like listening to the other guys tell their war stories. There is no better way to make a living.

And, you get to do important work. You get to make sense out of the world. That's a great thing—to make sense out of the world. When I was a kid, when I had no control, I had to invent my own sense, my own universe. There would be fights and chaos at home. Pop would be in debt and between jobs and my mother would be hysterical and I couldn't take it. Some days I'd just pack a lunch and get on the Long Island Railroad. Go out to those pretty suburbs and look at the schools with the neat lawns and playing fields and daydream that I lived in one of the nice houses and went to one of the clean schools. Some days, if I didn't have the money, I'd just start walking. Head out to the Island. Walk thirty miles and back. Just for the feeling of clean air and no fighting.

Becoming a cop was a little like that. I could arrange the world, settle fights, impose a little justice. I didn't have to run away to some fairyland of Long Island. I could control things right in front of me.

This is hard to give up. The control. No matter how bad you fuck up, you could always come back. You could always latch on to some hot case, break it, and become a hero. It's up and down, but this is how my career went. In the end, I had more than sixty medals on the racks running up to my chin. I could have had

*more, but I just didn't bother to write them up any-
more. No place to fit them. But it's still an honor. I still
felt a thrill of pride when I put on that uniform.*

*See, it's not all bullshit. Anyone looking at the
commendations knows that I am not one of those guys
who puts in eight hours and goes home. I'm not a paper
pusher. Anyone who looks knows that I am a real cop. I
am out there. I am on the fucking job.*

*One day, I had to go to court to testify in some case,
bullshit this or that, I'm not even on the job that long,
and I have the big rack of medals. I see this guy—a
motorcycle cop.*

*"You don't remember me, do you?" I ask this asshole
wearing all his fucking motorcycle leather.*

"No," he says.

*Well, I remembered him. It had been a while, but I
remembered. I was a kid, still in the academy. I was on
a date and he was a cop in Motorcycle Three in Queens.
He comes after me, pulls me over, right in front of my
date. Tells me that I ran a stop sign. I know that I did
not run the fucking stop sign, but never mind. "Listen,"
I say, "I'm in the academy. I'm gonna be a cop." The
guy still writes me up. Makes me look very bad in front
of my date. There's no professional courtesy there. Has
to be a real prick.*

*Now I run into this same asshole in court, six, maybe
seven years later. He's still a bullshit motorcycle cop
and I'm a fucking hero in the department, a fucking
legend. Everybody sees me, comes up to shake my
hand. Everyone knows me. I have no more room for
medals on my chest.*

*So I see this guy who wrote me up for passing a stop
sign and I say to him, "Hey, remember me?"*

He shakes his head. Arrogant fuck. So I say, "Well, I remember you and you're still an asshole; go fuck yourself!"

He has no idea what I'm talking about, but it felt good. It felt very good.

I never liked the traffic cops. They got a hard, fuck-your-grandmother attitude. When they have to make a quota, everybody goes into the fucking toilet. Heartless bastards.

Me, I had a tough time giving out tickets. Someone gives me a bunch of shit, they'll get a summons. But if he says he's sorry, I can't give him a ticket. Especially if he has kids in the car. I would never humiliate a man in front of his children. All he has to do is say he's sorry and have a bunch of kids sitting in the back seat and I let him go.

Writing traffic tickets is the worst part of the job. But sometimes being a cop is better than sex, better than food. And there are days like no other days.

Remember that day in October of 1977, when Reggie Jackson hit three home runs on three swings of the bat? He became Mister October. Three swings, three home runs. Lightning in his arms. I swear I know how he felt. I had days like that.

Me and Tommy had a streak—home runs every time we took a swing—right before the nun case.

There was a gang terrorizing the East Side. Knocking over Chinese restaurants all over the East Side of Manhattan. Must have hit thirty joints in one week. Same crew. Two Spanish and one black.

We weren't really involved because this is high-level task force work involving the Robbery Squad and I was a lowly anti-crime peon.

Nevertheless, I am aware that this shit is going on. This is the major shop talk in our part of town. One night, I'm in the Colonial on 116th Street and First Avenue with Tommy and Fish and a bunch of other guys having a beer and sandwich and we talk about this and that and then one of the guys at the table says that there was a stickup down the block earlier that day. Italian guy, eighty-two years old, who owns a fish market got hit. Imagine hitting an old guy like that? This guy starts describing the stickup team and it sounds just like the Chinese restaurant bandits. Two Hispanics, one black.

All of a sudden, I see an opening. Maybe we're not supposed to work on the Chinese restaurant bandits, but the fish store is in my territory. I listen, I make mental notes, and later, I begin to put out the word to my friends that I am interested in hearing about a three-man stickup team with two Spanish and one black.

The next night, a Chinese restaurant gets hit by the same crew, only there's an undercover cop planted in the restaurant. The three bad guys nailed him before he could go for his gun. They pistol-whipped him, beat the shit out of him, made him think he's gonna die. They ruined the poor fuck. Something happens to some cops when they're put in that kind of fear for their life. They can't go out anymore. Their hands shake. They sit in the locker room and cry.

I think of this and I think of these guys doing this to a cop and it made me a little crazy.

"Tommy, let's get these fucks," I say.

"I'll saddle up," says Tommy.

First thing we do is talk some shit to the kids on the street. They know me. They know I don't hassle anyone

259

unless I have to. I know that junkies were there before we came and they'll be there after we're gone. I do not regard drugs as all that serious a crime, unless they hurt somebody to get it. The things leading up to it and the things that stem from it are serious. These kids know that I have my priorities and they make me as a good cop. So my network of informers is out working for me. One kid on the street says to me, "Listen, Bo, I hear these guys come from Pleasant Avenue. One guy's name is Lawrence."

Now I am over on Pleasant Avenue talking to my people. I had a first name. I drive by a group of kids playing basketball in a schoolyard. Something makes me stop and walk over. I'm standing there by the fence and I call out, "Hey, Larry!"

This one kid, about sixteen, looks over. He's shooting a basket and he stops and looks over at me. I motion and he comes over.

"We wanna talk to you, Larry," I say. "Get in the car."

He throws the basketball back to his friends and he gets in the car and I know that we have one out of three. I can see it. First thing he says, "How did you find me?"

"Never mind that, Larry, we need the other two guys."

He doesn't wanna give them up. Fine. "You are going away for everything. Attempted murder of a police officer. You are going to jail forever, if you live that long."

He looks like he's gonna shit his pants.

"Look, Larry, we know that you're not the brains behind this," I tell him, because he's a kid. "We know that it was the other guys."

"Yeah, how did you know that?"

I get very hot. "Listen, you guys are making assholes

out of the police. How dare you rob thirty fucking joints in one week? You make us look like fools!"

He ends up giving up his playmates. He tells me that there's one guy over on Paladino Avenue and I go over and see him. I don't know if he's guilty or what. I only know what the kid tells me.

I go to this other guy, Garcia, and I say, "I'm Bo, the detective," and he knows who I am and I go into an act. "Listen, pal, you know that we have been having problems with these young kids breaking into cars." I say, "Listen, I have this car downstairs and I'd like you to check it out."

Meanwhile, I got a van at the curb with the cop who was beaten and one of the robbery victims watching through a one-way mirror. I am wired with a radio so that if he's the guy, they can tell me.

Garcia agrees to come down and check out the car and sure enough, when I walk him outside, I hear my guys give me the code. "Green light."

I grab him and run him across the lot. I want him off the street because his brother is the third guy. I take off with him.

How do I grab the brother? I leave word for him to call the precinct. I didn't say why and I've already grabbed the one brother. So, finally, he gets home and he calls the precinct and I go into another routine.

"Oh, hello, Joe, this is Detective Bo Dietl. You know who I am?"

He knew who I was. I say that I have a bullshit complaint here and I am trying to close out the fucking case and I would really appreciate his help. Some kind of unauthorized use of a car. The trouble is, I need his signature. Can't close out the case without his personal signature on the card. I make it sound like total bullshit; I'm really not interested because I have much

261

more important things to work on, serious stuff, so get your ass in here because if I have to go out there and bring you in, I'm going to kick some ass.

"Well, I can't come in right now."

"Listen, I told you. If I have to go after you, I'm gonna knock you on your ass. So walk it in here."

Bang!

And he does. He comes in, thinking this is some bullshit. I get him in the elevator and I have the witnesses out front and I get the word—we got the third guy. They all identified him.

They all went away for twelve years.

Now I get a letter from the chief. Great work.

At the same fucking time, we wrap up another case. This is a murder on the subway. Some guy stabs another guy on the platform at 116th Street and we get a radio call and we roll. Down Lexington Avenue, three stops, to head off the train. All we have is a description. Black guy, about five-feet-ten, wearing a baseball cap. Bingo! We grab a suspect off the train, rush him back, throw him in a lineup, and we got the killer.

The streak isn't over. There was a crazy bandit hitting all the McDonald's in East Harlem. Guy with a ski mask and a gun. He had everybody terrorized. He was fucking with us.

Now, on this night, Tommy and I had brought in a stickup guy with a shotgun and a .45 automatic. We have him in the stationhouse. He pulled his job outside the precinct, but we pulled it over to our precinct.

All of a sudden, it comes over the radio. "Tenthirteen, man shot, chase going on. One Sixteenth and Pleasant Avenue."

I leave the prisoner in the cage and go shooting over to the area. There's a couple of uniformed guys there and I ask what happened. "He went into that building there, Bo."

It's a big apartment building. I run up sixteen flights of stairs like a bullet. I'm not even thinking. There's a hall door leading to the landing and I open it and there's the fucking guy with the gun in his hand. He turns and starts to run. I had my gun in my hand. I could have shot him, right then and there. But I looked down at my gun and said, "Oh, fuck, here we go again," and I put my gun in my waistband and start chasing him down the stairs. I don't know why I didn't shoot him. I mean, he just shot someone. The guy's one flight ahead of me and I'm yelling down, "He's coming down, he's coming down," hoping there's gonna be some cops coming up the other way.

Bobby Marchant, who's a lieutenant now, hears me yelling and he's coming up, but the guy goes running right through him. He tried to shoot Bobby. They're in a big fight when I come running down. Everybody's fighting for the fucking gun. This guy is tough. He still had his gun and he's trying to shoot everybody.

Finally, I kicked him in the balls, which tends to freeze the action. I kicked him hard, like hard enough to take his balls off. Then I fucking smashed the portable radio over his head. We dismantled this fucker.

Ends up, he's the ski-mask bandit. He has four other convictions for bank robbery in federal court, along with several attempted-murder convictions. He gets four consecutive life sentences.

During the trial, when we were in court, the assistant district attorney comes over to me and says, "Bo, this is a real bad dude."

"I know. I was on the landing when he was trying to kill everyone."

"Bo, he's probably going to try and escape. He's got four life terms and nothing to lose."

I start hanging out after my testimony, on my time. Me and Bobby. Sure enough, on the last day, we are standing outside of the courtroom, looking through the window, and he peels off a pair of pants. He's got dungarees underneath the jail pants. He jumps over the rail and tries to make his escape. The judge goes under his fucking bench. Everybody starts screaming.

This guy is headed for daylight. He didn't know we were out there. We go charging in and catch him in midair. He sees me and goes, "Oh, no!"

But he's still fighting. Three court officers go out on three-quarters pay. Meanwhile, I take a shot at him and hit a steel girder.

Again, I kick him in the balls. They actually had to remove his balls. I said, "At least there won't be any more scumbags running around with his traits."

The supreme court judge sends a letter of commendation, speaking of our remarkable bravery. Remarkable police work.

This is right before the nun case. I was on a real streak. I felt terrific. Everything I hit was a home run.

But not with the chiefs. I'm a hero to everyone but the police brass. They criticize the fact that I didn't call the kids' parents in the Chinese robbery case—with a juvenile, you're supposed to bring in their parents before you question them. They don't like the fact that I took the McDonald's guy's nuts off. Never mind that I would have been justified in killing the fuck.

It's exhausting. I lay in the hospital in California with my busted leg, I feel this overwhelming exhaustion. Maybe I can defeat all the bad guys, but how am I gonna defeat the brass?

The Palm Sunday case still rankled. And there was that other stone: the memory of the nun case. Veteran detectives, as well as senior commanders, would believe until their last breath that Bo withheld vital clues from them in order to steal the glory. There was the enduring stigma of his Mafia connections. Bo didn't have a sixth sense; he had mob friends, they believed.

Chapter 27

It didn't take long before Bo became a hospital celebrity. The Arab royalty spread the word among the staff that Bo was a kind of law enforcement prince. Soon San Diego police officers came to visit in droves, and that, too, added to Bo's sense of sorrow.

As he lay there, with the cast running up to his thigh, Bo was confused. He didn't know in which world he belonged. Was the police department his true home, or did he belong among the entourage of the Saudis?

Whenever I looked up, I saw San Diego cops and the Saudis. They were the people taking care of me. I know that my guys are three thousand miles away, but this is what I see. That, and the big cast on my leg.

There was no question of a hospital bill. Prince Fahad paid for everything. Bo stayed in Fahad's twelve-million-dollar house. The prince had thoughtfully left behind the servants when he returned to Ranger school to pick up his diploma.

I had a lot of time on my hands. A lot of time to think. Am I gonna be able to do the job when I get back to work? Are they gonna put me on a desk? Is that my fate, am I gonna be a desk cop?

There's also the question of a pension. Your pension benefits are based on your last year on the job. So, if I earn more salary in overtime, I get a higher pension. If I spend a normal amount of time behind a desk and earn base pay, I am gonna make half of what I would make if I walk out after an active year.

But more than money, I do not like sitting behind a desk. I cannot make out a decent report. I am a street cop. But how can I be a street cop with a gimpy leg?

These things are running around my brain as I am living in this mansion in California, with servants running around getting me anything that I want. Prince Bo? Detective Bo? Or just plain Bo?

After Bo flew back to New York, he took his crutches and paid a visit to the Seven Five. The woman on the desk didn't know who he was.

He sat around the coffee room and heard some bad stories. Friends from other commands were broken for petty offenses. Even one of the heroes from the Palm Sunday Massacre was thrown off the force for having an interest in a business—the department did not approve. It did not look like a good time for Bo's friends.

It was always some boss shit. Little tyrants. They take a good cop and suspend him and take his pension away. I know that this is what they would like to do to

*me. I can't forget the words of Chief Sullivan: "He'll die
in Brooklyn." It didn't bother me too much before. I
could defend myself. But how can I defend myself, how
can I stage one of my magic comebacks with a bad leg?
I was getting very depressed.*

One day, while Bo was still on crutches, Prince
Fahad called. He had gotten his diplomas, attended
all the military schools, and now he required an
appropriate celebration.

"Come, Bo, I need you."

They were staying at the Helmsley Palace Hotel.
Two whole floors. An endless train of room service
moving up and down, bringing food and liquor.

*The prince is all excited when I get there. "We are
going to celebrate," he says.*

"Oh, yeah. How?"

"By playing a war game."

"Me? On my crutches?"

"Don't worry. You will be the umpire."

*There is a mountain in upstate New York in which
you can stage a little war game. You shoot little balls of
paint at each other. If you get hit with the paint, you're
dead. The prince rents the whole fucking mountain.
Makes some calls, gets everyone else thrown off his
mountain.*

*The entourage is looking a little worried. They're not
in the same shape as the prince. I mean, this guy is a
rock. He does push-ups and pull-ups and sit-ups all day
long. These other guys eat.*

*Someone asks how we are going to stage this war
game, considering the fact that the only thing these
people carry in their suitcases are three-thousand-
dollar suits.*

"No problem," says the prince. He whips out one of those attaché cases. Hands one of his flunkies ten thousand dollars and says, "Go buy fatigues. Army fatigues and canteens and webbing and boots and hats. The works."

"What time shall I have the limousines pick us up?" asks another flunky.

"No limousines," says Fahad. "One cannot stage even a mock war from stretch limousines."

Out comes the attaché case.

"Rent three vans," he tells another member of the entourage. "Try for khaki, but we'll take dark colors."

"This has to look like a military maneuver," he tells me.

Meanwhile, he calls LaGuardia and has his plane juiced up. We are going to fly into this war.

So, now we start marching down to the vans. Twenty-five men, all in fatigues, calling cadence in the swank lobby of the Helmsley Palace Hotel. We looked like a well-financed band of terrorists.

The doormen held the door while we marched out to the vans.

The prince really liked to play the part. Finally, we get loaded into the vans, by the numbers, and we start rolling, heading out to the airport. The prince has a radio. He orders the vans stopped on the Grand Central Parkway. Everybody has to get out and do fifteen push-ups.

"Except you, Bo."

There they are, doing push-ups on the side of the fucking highway. Cars are slowing down. There's a lot of near-misses. It's a fucking riot.

Finally, we load up into the plane and head out to the mountain. It's all ours. Cost him twenty-five thousand dollars, but he has the whole mountain for the day. They give you these paint guns and you run around shooting everybody with blue.

Someone shoots the prince. I say, "Well," and he looks at me, and I say, "It's okay, they missed you. You're the prince."

Big surprise, the prince's army wins the war. I don't know how he's gonna make out in a real war, but in my war, he's gonna get the benefit of the doubt.

I got a cooler full of beer and I'm sitting on the bottom of this mountain sloshing beer. Great way to go to war.

After the war, we all load back in trucks and drive back to the airport and fly back to LaGuardia.

It was so sweet. We wake up and the prince says, "Let's see Manhattan." And we hire three helicopters and fly around the city. You get dizzy flying around the city on a quick whim. You get very fucking dizzy when money is no object and you can rent a mountain for a war game.

And then I had to go back to work.

They had Bo working behind a desk, just as he feared. Not that he could do much of anything else. The leg was slow healing.

It was one of those days. I was doing an early tour and I got off duty at six. But I couldn't get to my car. There was some kind of demonstration outside of the stationhouse and it blocked the parking lot.

There was a bodega down the street from the stationhouse. I limped down there and bought a six-pack and brought it back to the TV room. I really wasn't all that anxious to go home anyway.

So, I'm sitting there, drinking my beer, waiting for

the demonstration to end, shooting the shit with some sergeant. All of a sudden Herbie Hohmann comes in and his face starts getting red.

He starts yelling, "What the fuck do you think you're doing?"

And he grabs the beer can out of my hand and he throws it into the garbage.

"Hey, what the fuck's eating you?"

"You're not supposed to drink on duty," he yells.

"Well, I'm not on duty," I say. "Check the fucking roll call. I signed out half an hour ago."

"I don't want you drinking in the fucking station-house," he says, and now he's in my face.

"You're just pissed because I wasn't drinking with you."

He's yelling and turning purple and finally, it's not funny. "Get out of my face or I'll break your fucking head," I tell him.

He goes wild. "Did you hear that?" he starts screeching. "Did everyone hear that?"

No, no one heard a thing. "We were all looking outside at the demonstration, Lieutenant."

This is serious. He makes a report to division. Like they don't have enough against me.

This is bullshit. This is the last straw.

Who can say why I did what I did? Maybe I wanted them to stop me from quitting. Maybe I wanted them to run after me and say, "Look, we're sorry, we know that you're a great cop and we finally appreciate you."

That's what I wanted all along. Just some recognition. Some small something that going out and getting my head busted and getting cut up and getting arthritis sitting in miserable alleys all night was not stupid and useless. Was noticed with pride. I didn't do it for medals. I didn't do it to be a big hero. Not really. I did it because I wanted to be a great cop. The best cop. Not some piece of shit under somebody's heel.

I always thought, you do good work, it comes back. Like casting bread on the water. People treat me decent, I am going to go the whole nine yards for them. But where? Where was the respect? Where was the pat on the back? I'm like a dog getting kicked waiting to be petted. After you get kicked too many times, you say, "Enough."

And so I put in my papers. God, even to say it hurts. I put in my retirement papers and they did not—as I expected, as I secretly hoped—kick them back. No one came over and took me around and said, "Bo, Bo, it's all a mistake. Don't quit. We need you!" No. They didn't do that. They were relieved. The thorn was out of their side.

The department can be cold.

Usually, it takes six months to process retirement papers. Usually they make the process deliberate and slow so that a man can change his mind. In my case, they rushed the papers through in eight weeks.

It was a raw day in March of 1985 when I officially retired from the New York City Police Department. I remember the sun. It was a very sunny day. But there was no heat from the sunshine. Just that bright light that made me shiver.

I got up early, not that I had slept much. I went down to the basement, where I keep all the trophies. All the pictures on the wall. All the newspaper front pages with me walking in suspects. Packing my black leather bag with my guns. I had three .38s and one 9-millimeter automatic.

And my papers. All neatly filled out. I put it all on the seat of the car and pulled out of the driveway.

It was hard. When I got onto the Long Island Expressway, I felt something on my cheeks. It was tears. Imagine. Here I am, after making fifteen hundred felony collars, facing down I don't know how many guys with guns, getting mugged five hundred times, crying like a fucking baby on the Long Island Expressway. I had to pull over.

Some motorcycle cop pulls up behind me and comes over and starts to ask me dainty little questions. Like do-I-know-what-day-it-is kind of questions. He's testing my sanity, which I suppose you have to do if you see a guy pulled over and crying on the Long Island Expressway.

I showed the guy my shield and said I was fine, but he stayed there, staring at me, like he was waiting for some signal whether he should send for a tow truck or an ambulance. "Look," I said, "I'm fine." And he nods and doesn't move. Finally, I'm mad and I say, "Hey, fuck off!" And the cop leaves because, in the end, he's a cop, too, and he knows that sooner or later, half the guys on the force are gonna end up like me on the side of some highway, running out of heat.

I made it down to One Police Plaza. I got myself under control. And I didn't see anyone that I knew. I was afraid of that. If I saw an old friend from the academy or from anti-crime, I might break down again. I didn't want to break down again.

I go up to the retirement section and there's this woman sitting behind the desk. She's chewing gum and reading some magazine and she doesn't even look up when I hand her my papers. She just checks to see that everything is filled out and she still doesn't look up.

She takes my shield and tosses it into a drawer. I

*could hear it clang against all the other dead
shields.*

Then she takes my ID card. She stamps RETIRED *into
the plastic. It's one of those perforation stamps, the
kind that leaves little holes spelling out the end of my
police career. She might as well have been punching
holes in my heart.*

Epilogue

Bo Dietl's departure from the police department was not without pain.

Long afterward, there was still a pang beyond explanation.

I never really expected them to let me go. Not really. I always thought that they'd realize it was a mistake, that they'd ask me back. I still expect it. To this day. I wait for the phone to ring.

Bo opened a security and investigations firm named Beau Dietl Associates, but it wasn't the same as being a cop. He still carried a duplicate of his badge and a parking permit in his car. Bo found himself, after leaving the police department, chasing cheating husbands, hiring guards. He managed to upgrade the business to get involved in investigating criminal cases, but it was never the same as being a bona fide member of New York's Finest. However, he did hire his old lieutenant, Herbie Hohmann and Detective Sergeant Jimmy Shea after their retirement, along with many other good detectives.

About three months after I left the department, I was double-parked on Third Avenue. I had the parking permit in the windshield. Some sergeant from Internal Affairs comes over and he sees the permit and he asks for my badge. I say, "What for?" He says I better just cooperate or else he's gonna pull me in, lock me up, burn down my fucking house, whatever. All the bullshit threats that they use on cops.

It occurs to me that I don't have to be afraid of this shithead.

"Hey, I'm not on the fucking job, asshole," I tell him. "I am on terminal leave. So go peddle your shit."

Meanwhile, a sergeant from the One Seven comes along and sees what's going on. "Hey, Bo," he says. "How ya doin'?"

"Tell this asshole to go screw."

The asshole calls for backup and a lieutenant comes down from the borough. He sees me. "Hey, Bo!"

I felt some satisfaction.

Not unmixed. For though he was not subject to IAD discipline, he was reminded that he was no longer a cop. Not officially.

Bo still sees the old partners now and then. They have dinners. They drink and joke and tell lies and war stories. But it's not the same. It's never the same.

In 1986, Bo ran for Congress from his home district in Queens. He ran on the Republican ticket and met several times with Ronald Reagan in Washington.

He got a nice note from Prince Fahad wishing him luck.

Bo started the race as an out-and-out conservative, preaching hard-line law and order. He wanted to slash big government and boost military spending and crack down on criminals.

But something happened during the campaign.

I'd go out to these nursing homes in Far Rockaway and I'd see how bad it was for the old people. I'd see how they didn't have enough money for medication, that they had to bankrupt themselves to live. It wasn't right. I wanted to do something about that.

The tone of Bo's campaign began to shift and he began to sound like a liberal Democrat. Bo then had a confrontation with the incumbent junior senator from New York, Alphonse D'Amato, because D'Amato would not endorse Bo and supported his opponent, Rev. Floyd Flake, for the black vote of Queens.

He wouldn't endorse me. He was supposed to, but he wouldn't. I grabbed him on a platform and I called him a little————. Which is what he was.

He really looked scared. I think he thought I was going to hit him. The little————.

Bo lost the congressional race, but he got more votes than any Republican ever won in that heavily Democratic district.

In January of 1987, Frank Dietl died. It was a long illness and there was a lot of suffering. Bo brought his father's body back from Florida, where he had retired.

They held the funeral in Queens where everyone knew Frank Dietl.

At the wake, Bo stood in front of the casket. He kept staring at his father's hands, gentle now, quiet now, a crucifix draped over them.

"Look at that," he said, nodding at the hands. "Look at the size of my father's hands."

One day, about a year after leaving the police department, Bo Dietl was sitting at his desk in his home in Ozone Park, going over the accounts for his private business. When he looked out the window, he saw someone acting funny. Walking back and forth in front of a neighbor's house, then trying the front door.

When Bo saw him doing the same routine at a second house, he ran out his front door in his bathrobe. He grabbed the stranger in front of a third house, taking away the dagger the man had in his waistband. The man turned out to be wanted on several burglary cases.

Chalk up one last arrest for Bo Dietl.